A SHORT HISTORY OF
Richmond Racecourse and its Grandstand

BY PROFESSOR MIKE HUGGINS
AND THE RICHMOND BURGAGE PASTURES COMMITTEE

A SHORT HISTORY OF RICHMOND RACECOURSE AND ITS GRANDSTAND
Richmond Burgage Pastures Publishing

Burgage House
1 Millgate
Richmond
North Yorkshire
England
DL10 4JL

ISBN – 978-1-5272-8649-8

Copyright © 2021 by Professor Mike Huggins and the Richmond Burgage Pastures Committee

All rights reserved. No part of this book may be reproduced in any form by electronic or mechanical means, including information storage and retrieval systems, without permission in writing from the publisher, except by a reviewer who may quote brief passages in a review.

BOOK DESIGN – YVONNE FINN – YFINNGRAPHICDESIGN@GMAIL.COM
COVER PAINTING – CATHERINE ALDRED – CATHERINEALDRED.CO.UK – ORIGINAL PEN AND INK ILLUSTRATION PAINTED IN WATERCOLOUR
DRONE PHOTOGRAPH, INSIDE FRONT COVER AND FRONTISPIECE – GUY CARPENTER – GULLWINGPHOTOGRAPHY.CO.UK

A SHORT HISTORY OF
Richmond Racecourse and its Grandstand

INTRODUCTION

Richmond Racecourse – Derelict Grandstand (R) and the Zetland Stand

The catalyst for this *Short History of Richmond Racecourse* was the belief of the Burgage Pastures Committee that the racecourse buildings had been wrongly included when the site was placed on the Common Land Register in 1968. In support of their application to deregister the buildings the Committee approached Dr Mike Huggins, Emeritus Professor of History at Cumbria University and a world authority on racing and racecourses, to commission a piece of work from him about Richmond Racecourse.

Part 1 of this *Short History* is structured around Professor Huggins's account of the history and importance of Richmond Racecourse and its buildings, most especially the grandstand. To his account have been added a few stories about the races that took place, some events and some of the colourful characters linked to the history of the racecourse.

Professor Huggins's work took the history up until 1892, by which year race meetings had ceased on the site. **Part 2** continues the story up to the present day. In addition to the historical narrative it provides a short account of the former racing stables in and around Richmond; it describes the range of activities that took place on the site once race meetings had ceased, such as golf and the annual military camps; it also recounts major events such as the viewing of the total eclipse in 1927 from the racecourse and the more recent Kite Festival (a fundraising event in aid of the repurposing and renovation of Richmond Station into a charity-run social enterprise).

At the heart of Part 2 is the story of the grandstand since 1892. It tells of its use as an isolation hospital and as an observation post by the Royal Observer Corps in WW2. It also highlights the gradual decline of this unique building, its partial demolition and the fight by the Burgage Pastures Committee to save it for future generations.

Our research on the racecourse since 1892 uncovered a significant archive of photographic evidence about the military use. **Part 3** therefore expands on the racecourse as a military training ground, on its fascinating use by the Royal Observer Corps during WW2, and on the growth of the Gallowgate Camp, now the Gallowfields Trading Estate.

This *Short History* would not be complete without an account in **Part 4** of the medieval origins of the burgage holders, their place in Richmond's history and the role of the Burgage Pastures Committee. Since 1853 it has been this Committee that has been responsible for the racecourse's management and its evolution from a sporting venue to a site that is best known today as a place for exercise and dog walking. Part 2 of the *Short History* also includes the story of how the Burgage Pastures Committee intervened in 1970 to help save the grandstand from total demolition and, in 2008, assumed full ownership of the racecourse and its buildings from Richmondshire District Council.

Its legacy of involvement over the centuries helps the reader to understand the efforts of the Burgage Pastures Committee since 2008 to improve the site and to restore and re-purpose the grandstand. The Committee believes that the grandstand, standing isolated and derelict, deserves to be restored and recognised, not just as one of the jewels in Richmond's Georgian heritage but as a unique part of the history of horse racing, both locally and nationally.

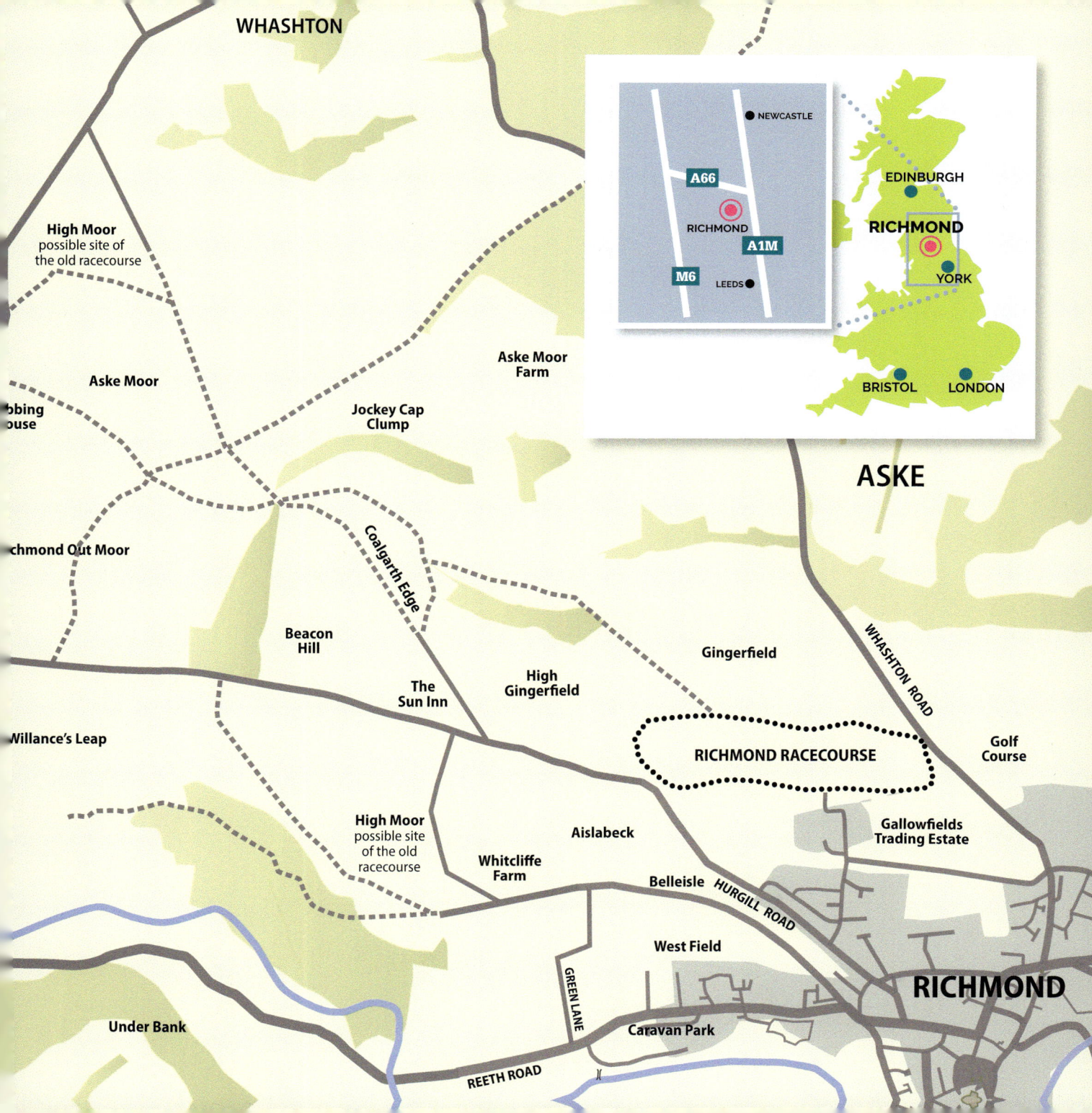

Part 1
THE SIGNIFICANCE OF RICHMOND'S GEORGIAN RACECOURSE

Richmond has a long history of breeding, training and racing British thoroughbred racehorses. Although today all that remain are the names of the training stables, such as Belleisle, and remnants of the racecourse and its associated buildings (the public grandstand, the Zetland Stand and the judge's box), the town is steeped in the history of horse racing. Richmond was the Middleham of its day, producing nationally famous racehorses such as Silvio and Voltigeur, winner of the Derby, the St Leger and the Doncaster Cup. Major races were held on its racecourse, such as the prestigious Richmond Gold Cup, attracting large crowds. The town's grandstand, still a dominant feature of the racecourse site, albeit in sad condition, is the world's oldest surviving stone-built public grandstand on a rural racecourse.

The very earliest reference to horse racing in Richmond goes as far back as 1512, from when there is an account of racing at Gatherley Moor, some five miles east from the town. By the time of James I the site had become one of the most celebrated places in the north of England for horse racing. Christopher Clarkson's *History of Richmond* describes a curious old racing song in a book called *Songs of the Chace* which begins with the words: 'You heard how Gatherley Race was run'. The Corporation Coucher Book of 1576 (in which the meetings and actions of the Corporation were set down) records a 'cup for the Horse Race in the possession of the Alderman'. The mention of a cup, possibly made of silver, would appear to be quite unusual as it was more common at this time to race for silver bells which could then be fastened to the brow band of the winning horse's bridle.

For much of the racecourse's early history, horse races in Richmond took place on the turf of the High Moor, close to the old road to Marske, although the actual location is ill-defined (See end notes, p77). The 1622 Coucher Book entry records 'a new maid race upon Rychmond Moore of iii myles which was contested by 6 horses' and that James Raine, Alderman, with his brethren had 'maid up a sume of xii poundes for to buy a free cupp'.

The entrance to the High Moor site is thought to have been beside the old Sun Inn, now demolished, where racegoers could quench their thirst. Some accounts of the site of the old racecourse use the term 'the Out Moor'.

Each year the town Chamberlains would organise the races on the High Moor. They would delineate a course on the open space of the moor with white tapes, record the entries for each race, set up starting and finishing posts, and arrange for admission money to be collected and for some means of checking the weight of the horses. Christopher Clarkson's *History of Richmond* (1821) describes how the course was 'sett forth and measured by Mr. James Raine, Alderman, and Mr. John Metcalfe, and many other gentlemen and good-fellowes the xxix of Aprill An.Dom. (29th April) 1622, with (the races) being run the vi (6th) of May.

It was not until 1765 that the venue moved to its more convenient and formal location on the Low Moor, where public races continued until 1891.

One of the most famous races that took place on the High Moor is commemorated by the Snow Tankard that was presented to Richmond Corporation. It is inscribed 'Gift of Sir Mark Milbank Bart and John Hutton Senr. Esq. To ye Corporation of Richmond after a disputed race in a great snow at Easter'.

The Judge's Box and in the background, The Grandstand

A SHORT HISTORY OF RICHMOND RACECOURSE AND ITS GRANDSTAND

> The story is that the horses of the two gentlemen were racing off against each other on the High Moor when a sudden snowstorm prevented any impartial witness from seeing which horse had won. Rather than either man accepting the prize wagered, nor wishing to race again, the two agreed to spend the monies on a fine piece of silver to be presented to the Corporation.

The Borough's own records state that the tankard was made in York in 1686 by the leading York goldsmith Marmaduke Best and that the race took place at Easter that year. It is probable, however, that the tankard was made even earlier. The prominent Richmond historian Ralph Waggett gave a date of 1615 for the tankard. Recent evidence that has been uncovered also casts doubt on the date of the race itself (see end notes, p78).

The Snow Tankard

The Snow Tankard, standing seven and a half inches high and weighing 32 ounces (19 cm and 900g), is one of the oldest sporting trophies in the country. During the 1980s it was displayed by the Victoria and Albert Museum in London in its exhibition of sporting trophies. It is now stored in the Green Howards Museum, Richmond, as part of the collection of Town Council Silver.

After a gap caused by the Civil War, racing returned to Richmond at the Restoration. *The London Gazette* from that period contains regular references to racing at Richmond. This alone shows the national importance of the town's race meeting. Most meetings took place in September, to coincide with the big cattle and horse fairs. *The London Gazette* of 2 August 1669 reported that 'a Fair has been granted to the Corporation of Richmond in the County of York, to be held from 13 to 16 September for beasts and sheep and horses. On the 17th of the same month, a horse race for a plate of £50 is to be run within the liberties of the said town of Richmond and the next day another by lower prized horses for a plate of £20.'

Queen Anne – 1665–1714

Queen Anne Cup

As the races grew in prominence, so the prizes became more valuable. In 1698 the Mayor and Aldermen collected a sum of money, including a guinea from the principal owners, as prize money for the races. In 1706, Queen Anne provided a gold cup to be run for at Richmond on 15 August by any horse carrying 12 stone. The Queen was said to have been very keen on racing and presented a number of gold and silver cups. The 'Queen Anne Cup' presented to Richmond, made by Pierre Harache II of London, is thought to be the oldest surviving example. Weighing some 23 ounces (650g), it is vase-shaped, with a moulded midrib on a stepped foot, with two leaf-capped scroll handles. On one side is engraved the Royal Arms of Queen Anne. On the other is an engraving of a jockey. The cup cost just over £122 when made. It was sold in 2001 from the estate of the 3rd Baron Rothschild for £223,750, having been given an estimated value of £300,000.

Christopher Clarkson, in his *History of Richmond*, describes how in 1753 the spirit of horse racing so pervaded the town that a collection was made to purchase plates for the races. The Members of Parliament for the Borough each contributed 15 guineas, every retailer of wine and punch erecting a hut upon the race-ground one guinea, every retailer of punch and ale 10s 6d, every retailer of ale only five shillings. This custom continued for many years and became known as the Town Purse. The account also points to the copious consumption of alcohol at the races, a tradition which is described in more detail later in the book.

It was in 1765 that the Corporation set out a new, more formal, racecourse on the Low Moor, not as far away from town and so more convenient for racegoers. The new course covered 82 acres, with an additional 44-acre training ground. The racecourse was a 1.5-mile course with a 5-furlong straight stretch. Work to level the ground and lay out the elliptical course must have taken some time, as well as expense.

So, the scene was set for the great era of horse racing in Richmond in the eighteenth and early nineteenth centuries, a story that is taken up in Professor Huggins's *The Town of Richmond and its racecourse*. His account has been enhanced by stories of some of the events that came to be associated with the racecourse at this time, such as the *Great Match (Glasgow Herald 1851/ Encyclopaedia of Flat Racing)* between Voltigeur and The Flying Dutchman, and the part played by Belleisle Stables in the gruesome murders by Dr William Palmer, the Prince of Poisoners.

The town of Richmond and its racecourse

The town of Richmond in North Yorkshire is privileged to possess what is now the oldest surviving stone-built public grandstand on a rural racecourse in the entire world, as well as an early judge's box and the remains of a late nineteenth-century stand, known as the Zetland Stand.

Contemporary evidence in the shape of a letter from a Richmond writer in 1776 clearly states that the grandstand was planned by John Carr (1723-1807).[1]

John Carr – by Sir William Beechey

Carr was the nationally-famous architect whose mixture of Palladian, rococo and antique-Roman building styles dominated building works across the north and midlands, paralleling the work of Lord Burlington and Robert Adam further south.[2]

Despite the major architectural importance of the grandstand, however, it is of even more significance historically and culturally in the history of horse racing. In 1775 the annual King's Plate at Hambleton, near Thirsk, was run for the last time, and George III decided that it should be run at York and Richmond alternately. This was a very high-status race, and almost certainly this was why Richmond rapidly needed the new grandstand for its first running in 1777. The Corporation also spent about £40 in further levelling and draining of the course.[3]

By the 1770s horse racing was recognised throughout England as the country's only fully national sport, and Richmond lay close to the heart of a relatively small thoroughbred breeding area in a region stretching from the Tees valley across to Helmsley and round to Bedale. This was nationally famous as the original centre of the development of the new hybrid form of racehorse, the thoroughbred, the subject of admiration, awe and wonder to sportsmen everywhere. Cricket was still largely confined to the south-east, and other sports such as pugilism, wrestling, pedestrianism and golf attracted only minor regional interest. By contrast the advertisements for and reports on the leading race meetings at places such as Richmond, Newmarket, Chester and York could be found not just locally but in the London, Edinburgh and regional newspapers right across the country. Richmond, like almost all other courses except Newmarket and York, then had a single annual race week.

To set this important site in context and convey its essence the following sections explore in more detail the grandstand, judge's box and Zetland Stand and their curtilages, as well as the social importance of Richmond and the introduction of the thoroughbred horse.

The first temporary stands

For many hundreds of years the only way to get a better view over the crowd at rural sporting events was by standing on a vehicle, climbing a tree or going further up a nearby slope. But as racing evolved, entrepreneurs began building temporary stands for the race week and charging admission. These stands were of wood, sometimes just rows of steps, called 'standings' or 'scaffolds', often open to the elements. These were erected before race week and taken down afterwards. These scaffolds were found in Richmond, as elsewhere during the eighteenth century. The Richmond Corporation Coucher Book shows the Pasture Master paid out money for setting up scaffolds, for posts and for cording the course in 1754 and 1755, while in 1759 two local men erected a scaffold 20 yards long and paid three guineas to the Chamberlains for the privilege.[4]

The emergence of the first permanent public grandstands in England

The really-rich wanted more exclusivity, privacy, shelter from the weather, and a more permanent stand. At Newmarket the brick-built King's Stand, much-painted by artists, dates from this period.[5] In about 1760 the Duke of Cumberland's stand was also built.

Up to almost 1750 there were no permanent public grandstands with shelter inside. But in about 1747 there was an innovation in Yorkshire, then the leading horse racing region: a new form of sophisticated recreational architecture for the better-off, the country gentry and leading townspeople. The first permanent small public grandstand in the world, in the modern sense, with imposing first floor and roof viewing platform, was built at Wakefield's racecourse, almost certainly planned by young John Carr, who then lived nearby at Horbury.[6]

This quickly stimulated interest at York, second only then to Newmarket as a racing centre. In 1753 Carr won a competition to build a stand there, funded by a subscription organised by York Corporation. Each share of £5 gave a gilt token for free admission to the grandstand for 100 years. The 140 subscribers included the titled, landed gentry and squires as well as prominent York tradesmen and professionals. The impressive stand cost around £1,900 to build, but raised annual revenue by charging entrance fees for admission by those who could afford it. There were gate keepers to check tokens and sell tickets.[7]

In the 1760s and 1770s the innovative fashion spread. The third Yorkshire grandstand was erected at Beverley, the leading East Riding meeting, in 1767, built at a cost of £1,000 with costs defrayed by the sale of 330 metal tickets, with the Mayor and Corporation taking two and the rest bought enthusiastically by the local élite.[8] In the midlands there were small stands at Peterborough in 1766 and Lichfield in 1773, and the Duke of Portland's private stand at Newmarket in 1774. Stamford got a small stand by the winning post in 1766, and a second larger stand in 1776 with two floors.

Richmond's stand, initiated in 1775, was the very first North Riding grandstand. The following year Doncaster, attempting to rival York and Richmond, constructed a new racecourse on Doncaster Common and built a large grandstand costing around £2,600. It was planned by Carr, who was by now the leading architect in the north and was even elected Lord Mayor of York in 1770. Doncaster also increased the value of its Gold Cup, and introduced the first famous Classic three-year old subscription race, the St Leger. Midland rivalry in 1777 from Nottingham saw John Carr gaining a further commission there, designing assembly rooms and grandstand for an improved race ground, with money raised from subscribers.

Many Georgian grandstands were constructed in subsequent years. The fashion spread, to America, to India, France and Europe. But very few stands of this period have survived. Many were demolished when new grandstands were built. Some were destroyed when racecourses were used for building. A very few became farmhouses. The Duke of Buckingham's small 1773 private stand survives at Blickling; Peterborough's stand was converted into a dwelling. Carr's other stands have long been demolished except for one planned by him at Kelso in 1778 but not built until 1822. Only Richmond's now remains.

The building of the Richmond grandstand

The process for building the grandstand began at a public meeting held in September 1775 at which it was decided to build a permanent new stand 'upon some part of the race Ground of Richmond for the better accommodation of the ladies and gentlemen attending the Races' (North Yorkshire County Record Office: MIC 1318). It is probable that the building work began in 1776 once permission had been granted. The Coucher Book records show that, 'on January 9th 1776 (in pursuance of an application having been made), leave be granted to the present stewards of the races to erect a stand upon any part of the new Race Ground'. It was funded by local and regional five-guinea subscriptions, probably paid to the racecourse stewards, one of whom was Charles Dundas, of Aske Hall, the leading local landowner. Each subscription purchaser gained a named metal circular token which entitled the possessor to perpetual and transferable stand admission. The list of subscribers, with their amounts, still survives. In May 1777 an advert was placed by Charles Dundas in some editions of the *York Courant*, describing the new grandstand as 'very commodious and elegant', indicating that the building had indeed been completed in time for the first running of the prestigious King's Plate at Richmond which was held that year.

The grandstand cost rather less than York's, probably around £1,300, but was a very elegant classical building, two storeys tall. On the ground floor were probably rooms for various racing-associated functions, a card room and water-closet facilities. A reception room above, with fireplace and some furnishing, would probably have extended the length and breadth of the building, and gave a comfortable area in which to socialise. Races could be watched from the large arched windows or from the balcony that encircled the entire first floor. Steps to the balustraded roof gave access to an even better view of the entire course.

**The Grandstand – Richmond Racecourse
Illustration by John Harland**

The placing of the grandstand in terms of local topography shows very innovative thought by John Carr and his clients, and is something almost certainly unique to Richmond in the history of British racing. Throughout the past 300 years the standard placement of permanent grandstands has been adjacent to and facing the course, and to the right of the judge's box. This always provided a most satisfactory view of the last two furlongs of the race and finish, but no or fairly restricted views of much of the race for most spectators.

In total contrast the Carr grandstand is set at some distance from the judge's box in a very high position at the centre of the left quadrant of the course, looking straight along the narrow oval towards the south-east. To see the finish, spectators had to take an angled look to their right. In fact this brilliantly exploits the potential of the topography. In 1775 most races were of four-mile heats, almost three complete circuits of the course for each heat, and this placement of the grandstand allowed grandstand spectators to watch almost the entire race except for the couple of furlongs behind the stand. In a period before bookmakers, when bets were made between individuals, this allowed in-race betting. The Enlightenment aesthetic of appreciation of the Picturesque was almost certainly also important. The moor was a recreational space incorporating beneficial contact with nature, and the view from the grandstand is spectacular even today, looking across to the Hambleton Hills, to distant Teesmouth and to even more distant Hartlepool.

The judge's box

Even in the first decades of the nineteenth century many racecourses had a judge's box at the finish, sometimes open to the elements and made of wooden scaffolding.[9] A few country courses had only a winning post. Doncaster had a small octagonal box, with windows all round, as did Ascot and Aintree. This shape sheltered the judge and allowed him to see much of the course as well as the finish.[10]

At Richmond, the horses were probably weighed out there, briefly parading up the course towards the grandstand before the race, and weighed in after the race to ensure they met the weight allowances. Christopher Clarkson, in his *History of Richmond*, describes how the judge's box was used 'for the convenience of the Stewards, or persons appointed by them as tryers, to observe the weighing of the riders and to decide in what order the running horses pass the winning post at the conclusion of the race'.

Judge's Box

It is from this dual purpose that the description of the judge's box as the 'stewards' stand' in some of the correspondence concerning the buildings almost certainly originates.

Detail – W S Goodburne Plaque on the Judge's Box

Although of no particular architectural merit, Richmond's late Georgian judge's box is the oldest one currently known to survive. It was built in 1814 at a cost of £200 and the still-surviving attached iron plate's inscription shows it was 'Erected 1814 by W.S. Goodburne Esq. Mayor'. The local historian Christopher Clarkson, writing in 1821, believed that the money came more generally from the Corporation, and that it was built by 'an ingenious architect of the place'.[11] It had a simpler shape, rectangular, with a Grecian roof and cornice, and had a semi-circular railed apse in front to allow the judge to look down the course, and was built of stone. It had a fireplace so it could be heated. Clarkson described it as 'a neat, square building, with a Grecian roof and cornice, battering out at the bottom, so as to give that strength and solidity which may enable it to withstand its high and exposed situation'.

The Zetland Stand

Plans for a handsome new stand were approved by the Corporation and burgesses in May 1883. The stand was proposed by Lord Zetland and other élite supporters of the meeting, almost certainly because the grandstand spectators were by then no longer of a type they and their wives and families found acceptable. It was built by private subscription. Tenders were put out, and Darlington architects Clark and Moscrop supervised its erection.[12] It seems to have been completed in time for the September races, and, by the following year, it and the grandstand were cleansed, minor repairs done and painted.[13]

It is this building, standing adjacent to the main grandstand, which became known as the Zetland Stand.

The Zetland Stand

The rubbing house

The Judge's Box and Old Rubbing House – The Illustrated Sporting and Dramatic News – December 1891

In the eighteenth century, for many races at courses such as Richmond, mature horses aged five or over often had to win two heats of four miles in order to win the race. Between heats they would be rubbed down and scraped with wooden scrapers or straw to remove the sweat, in a 'rubbing house'.

There is no surviving rubbing house on the Low Moor course, so it was probably constructed of wood. The site of an earlier stone rubbing house is still marked on Richmond Out Moor, just to the south of the High Moor, near Sturdy House Lane. The remains of this building now form part of a domestic dwelling which is named 'The Rubbing House'.

The rubbing house could also have been a testimony to a practice sometimes referred to as 'Yorkshire Sweating Gallops'. Trainers found that their horses built stamina, fitness and strength by losing weight through intensive work on the gallops. Yorkshire trainers were notorious for this practice in the eighteenth century and other training areas copied it. As race distances grew shorter and more races were for two-and three-year-olds, so it became clear that too much intensive work was deleterious and the practice declined.

As well as being used as a rubbing house for horses, this building, according to Christopher Clarkson, was leased in 1750 by Ralph Close, to the Mayor and Aldermen for the use and shelter of lead miners.

There is a further local example of a rubbing house at Middleham (High Moor).

The social functions of the Georgian grandstand

The Georgian experiences of the Richmond stand would have been multiple and overlapping. It provided a place for the local landed élite and those socially ambitious local middling groups (Corporation families, merchants, attorneys, etc.)

Derby Day 1850s, by William Powell Frith

who could afford entry, allowing some limited social mixing and enabling them to see and be seen. Folk there were separated from the rest of the crowd, literally and metaphorically looking down on everyone else, while visibly demonstrating their presence and superiority. Stand architecture was a way of creating a significant and clear physical demarcation. The grandstand encouraged more women to attend race meetings, giving them opportunities for social interactions and status displays, including the wearing of the most fashionable clothes available. The county and town 'company' met there, social connections were established and, sometimes, even the finding of future marriage partners could potentially empower and enrich women's lives.

The horse was central to Georgian society in terms of social and economic transport needs, for cavalry use, and for leisure practices such as hunting, hare coursing and horse racing. Gaming, whether with cards or dice, or wagering on future events was also central, not marginal, to Georgian life, a key feature of the 'season' at London, Bath or Brighton, and this was another major reason for horse racing's widespread popularity. The first bookmakers in the modern sense, offering odds on all horses, did not emerge until around 1800. In 1776 individuals in the stand would orally offer or 'lay' odds on a particular horse. A potential 'backer', hearing this, would attempt to take those odds for a particular sum, in the presence of others. The two usually noted the details in their small 'betting books', and would settle up debts later. Much of the betting by the titled and gentry at this time was deep play for very high stakes, anything up to 1,000 guineas or more, sending out cultural messages about status, courage, honour, wealth and risk-taking. It could sometimes be extravagant and reckless and lead to loss of estates. The stand was thus noisy with conversations and wagering between and during the races.

The grandstand offered political opportunities too, not just for the exercise of patronage, but also electioneering, political canvassing and lobbying. With so many of the landed élite present the stand provided a focus group to test out political ideas. But while the atmosphere of the grandstand was supposedly one of Georgian civility and politeness, this is unlikely always to have been so. There was huge excitement during an actual race as people roared on the horse they had backed. There were quarrels too, not least when betting disputes were involved. And not all the 'gentlemen' in the stand were gentlemen. Professional pickpockets could ape the clothing, speech and language to seize their opportunity as they moved amongst the group. Richmond's stand also had a limited multi-functional role at other times for organisational meetings, or watching military parades and displays and other sporting events.

Richmond Racecourse and some celebrated characters

Richmond Racecourse has been associated with some celebrated characters over the centuries. Here are the stories of two of them and their notable activities. Today, you can always find walkers out on the site of the racecourse, many of them with their dogs. None of the present day walkers, however, would contemplate the feat of John Batty in the late summer of 1788.

This was a period when wagering against time and distance walking was very popular and attracted many spectators. Where better to attempt such a wager than on the fashionable racecourse of Richmond, which was also used for other sporting events. So it was that John Batty, a poor local pig driver in his mid-fifties, placed a bet of 20 guineas to 100 that he could walk 700 miles around the racecourse in fourteen days. Although he must have been accustomed to long walks driving his pigs, this would require Batty to walk 50 miles every day for a fortnight.

Not only the distance and time of the wager posed a challenge to Batty. As a poor pig driver, he did not have more than one guinea of his own to put up against the wager. For this reason several of those that he wanted to have bets with declined the wager. Batty was forced to join in with others to raise the stake money, so agreeing to share out the prize should he win. He even had to resort to staking a sow against ten guineas.

Cheered on by a number of inquisitive local inhabitants, Batty went on to walk the 700 miles with five hours to spare. Even so, it was an object lesson in determination and single-mindedness. He had to suffer thirteen days of acute discomfort, having lost the skin off his feet after the first day because of new shoes. Nor did he gain huge rewards for his Herculean efforts. After sharing his winnings with those who had helped to put up the stake money, Batty took home sixteen guineas from his fortnight's labour out of the 100 guineas winning purse. When he bet that he could do the same again in thirteen days for 100 guineas, which would have been riches indeed now that he had the stake money, there were no takers!

Captain Robert Barclay Allardice

We have no picture of John Batty, but even more famous were the walking exploits of Captain Robert Barclay. He too had a Richmond connection and may well have been inspired by Batty's walk around Richmond racecourse. In 1787

Barclay came to Richmond School, at that time one of the most famous classical schools in the country, as a boy of eight. There is every chance that boys from the school would have formed part of the crowd who witnessed Batty's feat. In June 1809 Barclay became one of the most famous sporting figures in Regency times when he walked 1,000 miles in 1,000 hours for a bet of 1,000 guineas.

How to get a cheap ride

John Kilburn was a person well known on the turf as a list seller, that is to say he took race cards, listing the runners and riders, from local printers and then sold them on the course. One summer he found himself at a town in Bedfordshire and, according to a turf phrase, 'quite down', meaning that he had no money. It being the week before Richmond races, near which place he was born, Kilburn hit on the following expedient in order to arrive there on time. He went to a blacksmith of his acquaintance to stamp on a padlock the words 'Richmond Gaol'. The padlock was then used to fix a chain to one of his legs. Kilburn next went into a cornfield, supposedly to sleep. As expected, he was soon apprehended and taken to a magistrate. After some deliberation, the magistrate ordered two constables to guard Kilburn in a carriage and take him back to Richmond, no time to be lost, as Kilburn informed the magistrate that he had not yet been tried and hoped they would not let another Assizes pass by. The constables, on their arrival at the gaol, accosted the keeper with –

'Sir, do you know this man?'

'Yes, very well,' replied the keeper. *'It is Kilburn. I have known him many years.'*

'We suppose that he has broken out of your gaol,' said the constables, *'for he had a chain and padlock with your mark.'*

'A prisoner!' replied the keeper. *'I have never heard any harm of him in my life.'*

'Nor have these Gentlemen,' says Kilburn. *'They have been so good as to bring me out of Bedfordshire and I will not give them any further trouble. I have got the key of the padlock and will not trouble them to unlock it. I thank them for their good usage.'*

Sadly, John Kilburn's luck did not hold out. He died in December 1796 or early 1797 (the records vary) in very reduced circumstances. One version has him found frozen to death on the Great North Road between Stilton and Wansworth. A second set of reports has him dying in a pub at Water Newton, Huntingdonshire. All the accounts, however, describe Kilburn as well known to gentlemen of the turf.

Permanent curtilage

Georgian grandstands such as Richmond's normally had a further area around them enclosed by a low wooden fence. This curtilage at Richmond in the eighteenth century is likely to have taken a line similar to that of the modern circular pathway around the stand, rather than the recently erected fencing, thus allowing a view by grandstand spectators and the ability to walk round to see horses running behind the grandstand during the three circuits of the four-mile races. Within this select area spectators could promenade, socialise and talk to others outside the enclosed space between races. It is also just possible that, like York or Epsom at this time, it had a more rectangular wooden-fenced curtilage of some fifteen yards from the building all round. The curtilage subsequently seems to have varied, sometimes curved, sometimes straight. Photographs from the 1860s, for example, show a rectangular enclosure in front of the grandstand, marked by a wall topped by wrought-iron railings. Photographs of the Zetland Stand in the twentieth century show it had a separate wall and wrought-iron curtilage all round.[14]

The judge's stand was well away from the grandstand, and so the judge was liable to come under threatening physical pressure from more plebeian gamblers amongst the crowd lined up close to the finish, roaring their horses on and demanding a favourable judgement. In such cases the stand was likely to have had some limited railed enclosure around it of perhaps five yards with a gatekeeper to provide deterrence.

Semi-permanent and more temporary curtilage

From at least a week before the annual race meeting further areas of the course were always marked out and enclosed. Those wishing to sell food and drink or provide other facilities were expected to pay into the race fund which covered prize money and running costs, and were then allocated site positions on the course according to the amount paid. Local innkeepers usually played a key role. In 1824, for example, the Turf Coffee House, the Unicorn, Black Lion and the Red Lion each paid a guinea, the Talbot £1, while the Nag's Head, the Ship, the Three Tuns, the White Hart and Bishop Blaize paid half a guinea. All of these had wooden huts on the course, varying in size and position according to their subscription and sometimes with upstairs viewing areas. Some of these may well have remained in place from year to year, as in some other places. The Town Hall Tavern, which gained much custom during race week, also had a hut.[15] Without archaeological investigation, their actual location can only be speculative.

Over time, tents began to replace the earlier wooden or turf-built buildings, as they could be used at a number of events through the year. By 1883 there were five large tents, in line, beginning at about 20 yards from the new Zetland Stand. The Red Lion paid £12 15s; the Wellington £8 8s; Bishop Blaise £6 6s; the Bridge £4 and the brewery £1.[16] From the early nineteenth century there was also a small betting ring, and in 1884 the betting ring was enlarged.[17] Its location is currently unclear but would have been close to the tents.

Why was Richmond so important around the time when the grandstand was built?

In the 1600s and for much of the eighteenth century Richmond was the leading town in the North Riding, dominating what was then called Richmondshire. Mapmakers such as Speed often included street maps only of York, Hull and Richmond in their Yorkshire maps. When Charles I was brought down from Scotland at the end of the Civil War he stopped at Newcastle, Darlington and then Richmond on his route south.

The eighteenth century saw what historians call an 'urban renaissance' amongst those important northern towns with more servants, surrounding gentry and titled landowners. Towns like Richmond asserted their social status and position, usually remodelling the townscape and adopting classically-derived architectural styles and robust mechanisms of social differentiation. They paid growing attention to leisure activities and other new cultural pursuits. Their town Corporations recognised the importance of local leisure and often provided financial support for local race meetings.

Richmond followed exactly this path. Despite a relatively small population - around 3,000 - it punched well above its weight. Powerful politically, it was a Borough sending two MPs to Parliament and its Town Hall then held the quarter sessions for the entire North Riding. Religiously it was the centre of an archidiaconal consistory court, where wills were proved, licences and faculties granted, and all matters of ecclesiastical cognisance dealt with. Much better quality Georgian housing in Richmond dates from this period. Bridges were built or rebuilt and roads improved. The town attracted visitors and involved residents through its wide range of leisure pursuits. The Town Hall was rebuilt in 1756, and had a large and elegant room where balls and assemblies were held. Richmond had elegant inns and taverns such as the King's Head, begun in 1725, and the Bishop Blaize. It had coffee-houses, two fairs and a weekly market. Its theatre was built in 1788. It had a walk and promenade round its historic castle. Its bowling green was becoming unfashionable, but cockfighting mains, usually between the 'Gentlemen of Richmond' and the 'Gentlemen of Barnard Castle or Darlington', retained regular popularity until the 1770s, and at Martin's pit in Richmond in 1805, a main was attended by a 'large number of gentlemen from different parts of the kingdom'.[18]

Almost all such towns ensured they had a modern, up-to-date racecourse, recognising that it brought great advantage and profit to many of the town's citizens. York's Corporation, for example, had encouraged the removal of its course from Clifton Ings to the Knavesmire in 1730 and improved the track continually before the building of its 1754 grandstand.

Richmond did the same. In 1765 the town transferred racing from the course on the High Moor to the Low Moor, laying out gallops, clearing the ground and inserting posts. This began a new era of higher-status racing. The undulating course was levelled and drained where possible and put into initial good order. The Richmond Coucher Book shows the course was maintained by a permanent groundsman, was corded for meetings and had standings and scaffoldings.

Richmond and the thoroughbred horse

Racing at Richmond was of particular significance because it was in the area around Richmond and the nearby Tees valley that almost all the foundation mares and stallions related to the future thoroughbred were either bred or at stud at relatively small breeding studs at locations like Marske, Sedbury and Easby.[19] Horse ownership was central to élite Georgian society. When Daniel Defoe toured England around 1700 he emphasised that all the best and most costly horses for hunting and racing were bred in the North Riding and it was there that the best horsemen, horses and horse breeding were concentrated. He saw at Bedale what he thought were 'some of the best horses in the world'.[20]

The early eighteenth-century discovery that crossing the best North Riding-bred mares with the best imported stallions from Turkey, the Arab states and the Barbary Coast created a new, speedy and powerful hybrid, the thoroughbred, revolutionised élite racing. Richmond was right at the centre of this small geographical area where breeding first advanced, as 'Arabian' stallions were crossed with mares in traditional landowning families' small local studs, and modern thoroughbred horse racing first evolved.

The impact of the thoroughbred was substantial. In the period up to the 1750s there were many well-known thoroughbred breeders based round Richmond, such as the Darcy family, John Hutton at Marske, Simon Scrope at Danby Hall and Thomas Meredith at Easby. Richmond was also important in terms of racehorse ownership since the area possessed many racehorse owners of wealth, rank and influence such as the Dundas

Horses Exercising – The Illustrated Sporting and Dramatic News – December 1891

family, with great houses, large stables and estates. Racehorse ownership had particular concentrations around London, Newmarket and Yorkshire, most especially Richmond, Bedale, Beverley and Pontefract. The high-bred thoroughbred horse, the most successful in racing history, was rare, expensive, of real status and in huge demand. Winning races, gaining cups, plates and prize money, conferred great status on a horse's owner.

As thoroughbreds evolved between the 1680s and 1750s owners became well aware that their prized horses needed to be trained and ridden by expert jockeys and trainers, employed for the purpose. They also began to understand that their horses raced best, not on owners' estates on flatter ground, but when given sustained training gallops on good turf, up hills as well as on the flat, to extend their capabilities without the risk of injury. Even as early as the beginning of the eighteenth century, the ideal, peat-based moorland at Richmond, Middleham, Hambleton and Malton was being already used to provide owners' horses with more strength and stamina, and stables rented to accommodate them and stable staff. Right through the eighteenth and for much of the nineteenth century there were well reputed Richmond trainers with large stabling based at locations such as Belleisle, Silvio House, Temple View or Aske Hall.

The duel

Sometime around 1780 - the actual date is difficult to establish - an affair of honour took place on the racecourse. This took the form of a duel between a Captain Dawson and John Wycliffe.

What little is known about Captain Dawson is that he lived in the first house East Row, North End, Millgate, Richmond. The house was owned by a George Gill. Today, it is the offices for the solicitors Hunton and Garget.

More importantly for the cause of the duel, Captain Dawson's friend John Wycliffe, with whom he was on the best of terms, formed an improper relationship with Mrs Dawson, who was described as 'a fine looking woman'. Dawson suspected that

Painting of early Victorian duel – Artist unknown

something was going on, but could not prove it until he picked up the remains of a torn love letter. He was able to piece together enough of the letter to convince himself of the affair between his wife and his close friend. With his honour and that of his wife besmirched, Captain Dawson immediately challenged Wycliffe to a duel. It was to be pistols at dawn on the racecourse.

What gives the story an added interest is that Wycliffe's second was Christopher Clarkson, author of the famous *History of Richmond*. The lives of all of the main participants were affected. Wycliffe was seriously injured in the duel. Though he lived for some time afterwards, the ball could not be removed. Captain Dawson immediately left Richmond with his family.

Christopher Clarkson had intended to take Holy Orders, but this was prevented by his role in the affair. He went on to serve in Lord Fauconberg's White Coats at the time of the American War of Independence and then in the North York Militia, before beginning his famous *History of Richmond*, the smaller edition of which was published in 1814 and the larger version in 1821.

The race week in Richmond in the eighteenth century

The key to a race meeting's reputation was substantial prize money. This attracted entries of the big-name racehorses that the people of a horse-loving county like Yorkshire wanted to go to see. Gold cups and the few royal plates granted by the crown were the most coveted trophies but few meetings had them.[21] In 1728 many races were still for small galloways or hunters, and were usually for horses aged five and over, and it was common for two men sometimes to match their horses against each other for wagers outside race week times. Most horses only ran at their nearby meetings. Few raced more than four times a year.

The two major Yorkshire meetings were at York and remote Hambleton, on an old drove road, which had the best turf in Yorkshire, but had limited inn accommodation. During its six days of racing York had a 100-guinea Royal Plate, attracting thirteen entries, and a Gold Cup of £60. Hambleton's Royal Plate, held during a two-day meeting, attracted fourteen entries. Horses were walked to these high-status meetings across country for substantial distances, down from Scotland and Northumberland or across from Lancashire.

In 1728 Richmond had a two-day meeting, with one heat race daily. (Such races were a common feature of race meetings at that time. Rather than a one-off race, horses would contest the best of several heats, all in the same day).

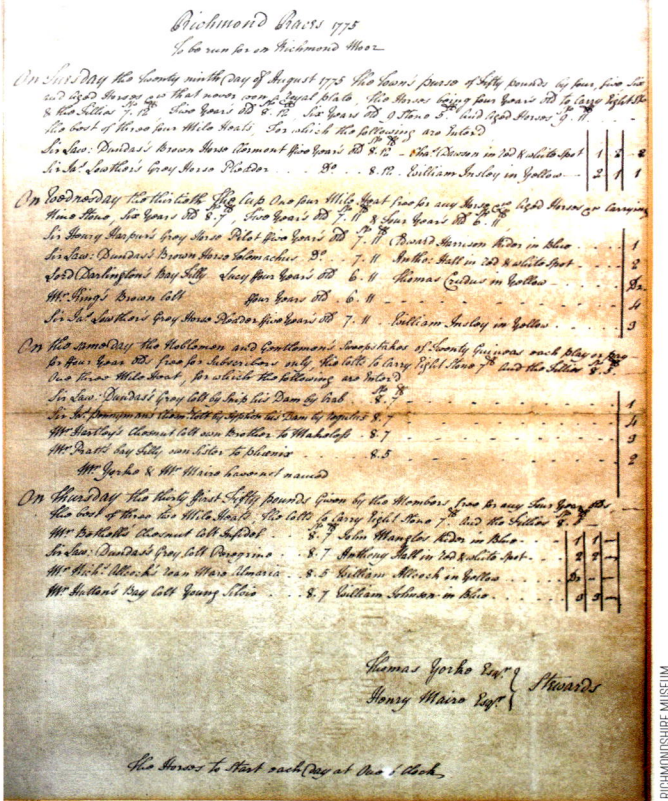

Race Card 1775

The first, for five-year-olds, had a substantial prize of 100 guineas. Racing was then on the High Moor. Nearby Bedale, Middleham and Leyburn also had races.[22] By the 1750s press reports regularly provided both results and betting odds at more major events. Between 1750 and 1800 only York was able to regularly provide entries for a six-day meeting.

The high-status meetings at Richmond, Beverley, Hull and Malton averaged three days, as did Boroughbridge and Northallerton later in the century.

From 1759 Richmond was ambitious enough to offer a Gold Cup and attract entries from leading owners such as the Duke of Cleveland and Lord Rockingham. The building of turnpike roads facilitated travel to urban meetings across Yorkshire, and made remote Hambleton, where there was nowhere for women to stay, much less fashionable. By contrast, the building of the Lancaster–Richmond turnpike in 1751 boosted Richmond's through traffic and trade and it settled on a September three-day race week.

Stamina was still a prized asset for horses. On Tuesday 6 September 1768, racing began with a single race, a Town Purse of £50 for the best of three four-mile heats, with rests of half an hour between them. So a winning horse would have had to cover twelve miles in total during the afternoon. On Wednesday, the first race was the best of three two-mile heats for four-year-olds for a purse of £50 provided by the two local Members of Parliament. A second race was a sweepstake, for three-year-olds, funded by the horses' owners, each paying 20 guineas, run over a single two-mile distance. On the Thursday, the first race was for the prestigious Gold Cup, over four miles, entered by horses of four years upwards. The meeting concluded with another sweepstake, of 20 guineas each from noblemen and gentlemen, over a three-mile distance. This was a modern programme for the time, when races for older horses, having to win the best of three four-mile heats, were still common. Sweepstakes and races for younger horses over shorter distances were only just becoming fashionable.

In their early days Richmond race meetings were badly attended and offered only poor prize money or, alternatively, cups and tankards such as the Snow Tankard or small pieces of plate. To increase the prize money the meetings were subsidised by the local aristocracy and businessmen, as in 1698 when the Mayor and Aldermen collected a guinea as prize

Thomas Dundas, 2nd Earl of Zetland (1841) by Francis Grant

money from the principal owners. These owners included the Dundas family from Aske, the Duke of Leeds, the Earl of Harewood, Mr Hutton from Marske and many more.

Richmond Gold Cup 1802 by Paul Storr

As prize money grew during the 1700s and races offered more prestigious cups, such as that donated by Queen Anne in 1706, so the meetings gradually became great social and romantic occasions and were picturesque, colourful affairs. Richmond Race Week had become a special occasion, to be looked forward to all year, and saved up for as the high spot of the year. The excitement would build up a week before the races began as racehorses began to arrive, walked to Richmond from their stables elsewhere. Once arrived, they were stabled and plated by those who had subscribed to the annual town collection made by race officials. Horses could also be watched exercising on the moor.

Wealthy families from all over the north would arrive in Richmond for the races in beautiful coaches and post chaises, attended by outriders and footmen all in colourful liveries. Postilions (coachmen who guided the horse-drawn carriages) would be in yellow jackets and decorated caps, and grooms in bright crimson livery. Ladies and gentlemen of fashion were stylishly attired and added to the pageantry of the occasion. Assemblies and balls were held in the Town Hall, hotels and private houses. Nearby country houses would be filled with invited guests. Some visitors would pay to take over a town house. Others took rooms in taverns and inns.

For the ordinary folk everywhere, there was a sense of festivity and general jollification. Samuel Butler and his travelling players would perform plays at the Georgian Theatre.

Illustration of early theatrical performance in the Georgian Theatre

There was boxing and cock fighting, card playing, drinking and gambling in public houses in the town. Huts for food, drink and gambling became available, decorated with flags, bunting and other signs. On the first day of the races, gigs and carts, coaches and other vehicles would arrive up on the moor, and many country folk, men, women and children, would walk into town from miles around. Meals, called ordinaries, held in local inns on the morning before the race, offered another opportunity for socialising, as did the evening assemblies at the Town Hall, where dancing, card play, eating, drinking and socialising went on well into the night. Drinking of alcohol at the races in the huts, booths or tents was as favoured an activity as wagering, and could lead to disputes and quarrels. Prostitutes, pickpockets and card sharps pursued a summer course from meeting to meeting.

Members of the public who had subscribed five guineas (about £1,000 in present day value) when the grandstand was built received a lifetime metal circular token for free admission to the building and others paid for a season ticket. This cost 10s 6d in 1820 (about £50 today).

Richmond racecourse became known as 'The Shire Capital of Turf Affairs'

Richmond Grandstand Subscriber Token

and it was said that there was no better place in the north 'to try the goodness of a horse's bottom'. The custom of collecting 50 guineas for one of the prizes, called the Town Purse, still persisted. The two most prestigious races were the Corporation Cup worth 60 guineas and the annual Richmond Gold Cup, worth 100 guineas, run in the autumn and attracting crowds of up to 8,000 eager racegoers. The race of four miles was generally run in seven minutes. The first Gold Cup race took place on the High Moor on 10 September 1759 and soon became one of the most prestigious trophies in the North of England. For the first five years it was won by the Duke of Cumberland's horse, Dainty Davy, and there was even a pub in Rosemary Lane called the Dainty Davy. In 1764, the last year of races on the High Moor, the Gold Cup was won by John Hutton of Marske's horse, Silvio. The jockey, Charles Dawson, retired on the proceeds and set up a training establishment, building a house which is still called Silvio House.

Every year between 1759 and 1858 new Gold Cups were awarded, many designed by the famous Scottish architect Robert Adam, and they would be placed in the window of the Mayor's house on the eve of the race. The silversmith was ordered to make the best Gold Cup he could for 100 guineas.

On the race day, the cup was decked with ribbons, then suspended on a pole and paraded through the town by the two Sergeants-at-Mace. They were dressed in formal regalia with antique cloaks, lace cravats and cocked hats. Not being horsemen by nature they rode large but extremely docile horses, lent for the occasion. Thousands of people, both locals and visitors, gathered in the Market Place to watch the parade, which left the Market Cross to the cheers of spectators. It then travelled along Finkle Street into Newbiggin before ascending Hurgill Road to the racecourse.

The cup was placed in front of the grandstand where it could be admired by the crowd. Once the race was over the cup would be presented to the lucky owner, filled with champagne, claret or mulled port. He would toast everybody from the jockey and trainer down to the stable lads, not forgetting the Mayor, the Corporation and the people of Richmond.

A regular supporter of Richmond's Gold Cup race was the Earl of Zetland, the Rt. Hon. Thomas Dundas, a well-known racehorse-owner, who arrived by carriage from his Aske Estate with due pomp and ceremony. His route would take him down Quaker Lane, where more spectators would gather to watch the cavalcade pass by. After 1883 he and his family would watch the races from his own private stand next to the main grandstand. The Dundas family still remain at Aske and have been closely associated with the Richmond racecourse to the present day.

In their heyday, Richmond race meetings were of great economic importance to the town. The racing stables provided employment, not only for the jockeys, stable lads, blacksmiths and saddle makers, but racegoers also needed coachbuilders, cordwainers (shoe makers), dress and bonnet-makers and tailors. The 'lower order of people' would walk for miles to Richmond and provided a welcome income for the local public houses and their semi-permanent huts on the racecourse that served food and drink for racegoers. In 1846 the railway was built, partly in recognition of Richmond's important position as a society centre and the significance of its race meetings.

Doctor Syntax – Painted by James Ward, 1820

Richmond Station Master's wife and itinerant buskers

A SHORT HISTORY OF RICHMOND RACECOURSE AND ITS GRANDSTAND

The story of the Richmond Gold Cup has been immortalised by the Richmond Folk Group, Fourum, in their song about this special fixture in the racing calendar. The pomp of the occasion and the role of two actual Sergeants-at-Mace, Neddy Marley and Bill Brown, is captured in the lyrics featured below.

In the Mayor's residence in
the day before the race,
The cup had been exhibited
to all the town
And now it was entrusted to
the Sergeants-at-Mace
Suspended on a pole with fine
ribbons hanging down
Ned and Bill in full regalia
looked a dashing pair
In their ancient cloaks
and lace cravats and cocked
hats on their head
As flushed with pride they raised
their precious burden to the air
They'd never been so well turned
out – the crowd all said.

Chorus
What a sight to behold
as they paraded down the road
The crowd all lined along
the route to cheer them
on their way
Neddy Marley and Bill Brown
were applauded through
the town
As they rode to Richmond
races on Gold Cup day.

At about the hour of noon
they began to celebrate,
By parading to the Market Place
and the crowd's great roar
And three times round the
Market Cross they did parade.
Down Finkle Street
and Newbiggin and up
to Richmond Moor.
From Aske Hall too the
Earl of Zetland came
to watch the race,
In a carriage with six horses
and outriders front and rear
There were gasps of admiration
and delight on every face
But when the cup came by
and caught their eye,
they raised the loudest cheer.

And now before the Grandstand
the cup was placed on view
While Ned and Bill watched over
it until the race was run
Then a roar went up and they
were off, and cheers
resumed anew
Then the cup was then presented
to the owner who had won
The champagne flowed in great
amounts and port and claret too
With toasts to all and sundry
who helped to win that year
For Ned and Bill their day of
glory now was nearly through
But as they ambled home
that night, the roar still
echoed in their ear.

Painting by Sally Zaranko from the book 'The Dales Collection' copyright Fourum Music

Racing in 1818

During the Napoleonic wars some courses struggled, but, while Richmond lost its King's Plate, it was still supported well financially by its Corporation, and its 1812 meeting was attended by all the principal families in the North Riding. By 1818 Richmond had gained reputation again and was probably at its zenith. It attracted the very best horses in the north, and people visited from across Yorkshire and sometimes beyond. Most races were sweepstakes, the earlier longer-distance heat races were disappearing, and more races were shorter-distance ones for younger horses. Tuesday 6 October 1818 had a sweepstake of 20 guineas for three-year-olds over a mile and a half, a sweepstake of ten guineas over four furlongs, and the Members' Plate of £50 - limited to horses that had never won £100 - which required the horses to win two two-mile heats (it took four heats to decide the winner). Wednesday had a sweepstake of 20 guineas each for three-year-olds once round the mile-and-a-half course; a 30 guinea sweepstake once round; and the Gold Cup over four miles, which attracted the two leading horses of the day. The winner, Dr Syntax, who won at least 36 races in ten seasons from 1814 to 1823, including many Gold Cups at Richmond, Lancaster and Preston, was owned by Ralph Riddell of Felton Park, Northumberland. Like most other horses of the period, having to be walked to all his meetings, he never raced more than six times a year. Blacklock, who won seventeen of his 23 races from 1816 to 1819 and was owned by Richard Watt, owner of the Bishop Burdon estate, came fourth. On Thursday there was a 20 guinea sweepstake for two-year-olds over four furlongs; a 30 guinea sweepstake for non-thoroughbred horses of ten guineas; a handicap stake worth £50 ; and a sweepstake of ten guineas with £50 added in two three-mile heats. Crowds at this time were often much higher than a town's local population, and at Richmond may have reached eight thousand or more.

Drunkenness and disorder

Richmond race meeting was an opportunity for raucous and rowdy behaviour, with copious and sustained drinking of alcohol fuelling the carnival atmosphere. Heavy drinking would begin in the local inns on the morning before the races. As the crowds then followed the Gold Cup on its ceremonial procession up Hurgill Road there were opportunities for more drinking in the 'pavilions' that had been set up or in pubs such as the Sun Inn. This was a pub that had a long association with Richmond racegoers. Located opposite the entrance to the High Moor course, it was still open when racing moved to the present course and would be well supported on race days. Drinking and gambling in the huts or tents set up around the racecourse would seem to have been as much a focus of the day as the races themselves. The grandstand itself was even licensed as a pub between c. 1822 and c. 1851. The extent of inebriation can be imagined from the account of a doctor having to use a stomach pump on one intoxicated racegoer.

At the end of the day's races, the crowds would stagger back to town to continue their drinking and to relive the excitement or disappointments of the day. As described in the poster (see right), the consumption of alcohol and its associated disorderly behaviour went on throughout the town, in pubs and private houses, well into the night. Places such as Finkle Street were clearly areas that no 'respectable' Richmond citizen would consider entering during the race meeting.

The poster itself, printed on behalf of a Richmond burgess in October 1844, reveals the growing tide of opposition from the more respectable classes and from religious leaders to the alcohol-fuelled revelry of a Richmond Race Day.

It did not even need a race day in Richmond to provide the opportunity and excuse for excessive drinking. Audrey Carr, in her book *You Must Remember This*, included an account from the *Darlington and Stockton Times* of 1898. The account looked back on the celebrations in 1850 when Lord Zetland's famous horse, Voltigeur, won the Derby. 'What a furore, what revelry, how strong liquors flowed like water when Lord Zetland's horse won the Derby. A pot of money made, maybe a wagon load came into Richmond, for everybody had backed their local favourite, and didn't they spend it. It was told

Official Town Notice cautioning those who were prone to over-indulgence

that about eight or ten of the old hands died off within twelve months of this great haul being made. They liquored day and night for weeks and their constitutions, not being as stable as the walls of Richmond Castle, gave way under the strain.'

The Great Match, 1851

On 13 May 1851, Voltigeur took part in the 'Great Match'.

The epic race took place at York racecourse, watched by a crowd that was estimated to be between 100,000 and 150,000. Many had walked all the way from Richmond to see their favourite, Voltigeur, or Volti as they called him, take on The Flying Dutchman in a challenge match arranged by their respective owners, Lord Zetland of Aske Hall, Richmond, and Lord Eglinton of Ayrshire. The purse was 1,000 guineas from each owner on a winner-take-all basis, the equivalent of £150,000 in today's money.

Painting by John F. Herring - this image became one of the most widely reproduced racing images of the time.

The rivalry between the two horses and their owners had begun the previous season. Having raced only once before, in 1849 as a two-year-old on his home course of Richmond where he won the Wright Stakes worth £65, an unfancied Voltigeur, trained by Robert Hill in Richmond and exercised over the racecourse gallops, had romped home in the 1850 Derby at a price of 16–1. He had then won the St Leger in a re-race against Russborough after the first race had been declared a dead heat. These wins were the prequel to a race against The Flying Dutchman in the Doncaster Cup. The unbeaten Flying Dutchman, trained at nearby Middleham, had won the Derby and the St Leger in 1849 and was the strong favourite at odds of 4–1 on, even though he conceded a 19 pound advantage to Voltigeur. The race went down in racing legend. The Flying Dutchman's jockey, Charlie Marlow, was still the worse for drink and set off too quickly. Voltigeur, ridden by Nat Flatman wearing the famous 'Aske spots', steadily caught him up and dramatically won the race by half a length. It was said that The Flying Dutchman's owner, Lord Eglinton, and the jockey, Marlow, were 'as pale as ashes'. It was the horse's first defeat in fourteen starts. Volti's supporters went wild with delight.

So it was that the two owners agreed to a re-match between their horses over two miles on the Knavesmire racecourse at York that next season. At stake was not just the huge purse but also the reputation of the two horses.

Emotions ran high with both sets of supporters. Those who came to back The Flying Dutchman had even prepared a poem for the occasion!

> *Ye backers of Aske's Voltigeur, boast not too much of his strength*
>
> *Though The Flying Dutchman lost the race, 'twas but by half a length*
>
> *Doubt as ye will, his heart is still as strong as Spanish steel,*
>
> *And o'er Knavesmire 'gainst that verdict he will enter an appeal.*

(from **Great Jockeys of the Flat** by Michael Tanner and Gerry Cranham)

When the flag fell, Voltigeur went off at the 'top of his pace' and took a lead of three lengths. Gradually, however, the heavy ground took its toll and, as they passed the stand, the horses were neck and neck in a 'struggle of desperate effort'. It was too much for Voltigeur and The Flying Dutchman passed the winning chair in the lead by a short length. So ended the 'Great Match', one of the most celebrated match races in thoroughbred racing.

50 years after the famous race, Voltigeur's beautiful 40-inch-long raven-black tail was still preserved in excellent condition in the saddle room of Aske Hall. A few years ago, the glass case in which various parts of the Voltigeur story are still housed was offered to and accepted by the National Horseracing Museum in Newmarket, thus exposing the story of the great match to a much wider public. Today, Voltigeur's name lives on in the 'Voltigeur Gate' into Aske Hall, the home of the Marquess of Zetland, and in a famous painting by the renowned artist, Edwin Landseer. This was the only portrait of a horse that Landseer painted. The artist was said to have been fascinated by the two cats who shared the horse's stable. The painting is still on display at Aske Hall.

Robert Hill (Trainer) and Job Marson (Jockey) with Voltigeur

Voltigeur – Painting by Edwin Landseer

Voltigeur's fame was also immortalised in another famous painting by English painter, William Barraud.

The Prince of Poisoners and Richmond Racecourse

One of Richmond's most famous training stables was at Belleisle, adjacent to the racecourse. It was here that John Gill, who took over in 1835, worked with Lord Zetland's famous racehorse, Voltigeur. The stables also have another, very different, claim to fame. In 1854, Belleisle was the location for a key episode in the gruesome murders carried out over several years by Dr William Palmer, the 'Prince of Poisoners'.

It was in the parlour of Belleisle that Edward Gill, who had taken over the stables from his brother John, negotiated the sale of two racehorses, Chicken and Nettle, to Dr Palmer, who had arrived there accompanied by a friend, John Parsons Cook. (John Graves, in his book on Palmer, gives a date of 1855 for the sale, but Fairfax-Blakeborough, based on the Tattersalls Newmarket Sales Book, records it as taking place in 1854). Palmer had become interested in horse racing some years before and had borrowed £600 from a Leonard Braden, a man he had met at the races. Braden then died in agony in Palmer's house in 1850. So his path had taken him to Belleisle, Richmond's famous racing stables, with his friend, John Parsons Cook, who shared Palmer's interest in horses and gambling.

The purchase price for the two horses was £2,500. Palmer even gave Edward an extra £100 as a token of goodwill, but Edward was not to know what consequences the sale was to lead to. It was a purchase that was to help take Palmer to the gallows.

William Palmer, The Prince of Poisoners

William Palmer had qualified as a doctor in 1846 and practised in his home town of Rugeley in Staffordshire. Palmer soon became associated with a series of unexplained deaths. First, there was a tradesman called George Abley who died after a drinking contest with Palmer in the Lion and Flag pub. Palmer was known to have taken a strong interest in Abley's attractive wife. Although Abley's sudden death and Palmer's possible motive were grounds for suspicion, nothing was ever proved. After all, Palmer was a trusted family doctor.

In 1847 Palmer then married Annie Thornton. His mother-in-law, also called Anne, who had inherited a fortune of £8,000 and was known to have lent Palmer money, came to stay with them in 1849. Her forebodings about living under the same roof as Palmer proved to be well founded. Two weeks after coming to stay, she died unexpectedly.

The deaths in Palmer's family did not end with his mother-in-law. Palmer and Annie had five children, but, between 1851 and 1854 four of the children died. Only one survived to outlive their father. The cause in each case was listed as 'convulsions'. High infant mortality was not uncommon at this time, but at his later trial there was speculation that Palmer had also murdered his children to save the cost of their upbringing. Then his wife, Annie, died in September 1854 after a short illness characterised by violent vomiting. Just before her death she had taken out a life insurance policy for £13,000. It was thought likely that Palmer killed Annie in order to claim her life insurance and pay off some of his gambling debts. To his wife was then added his unfortunate brother, Walter, who died in 1855.

Palmer's addiction to gambling only increased with the purchase of the two horses, but he was not successful and his debts grew ever larger. Palmer had twice been in the Defaulters' List for failing to pay debts. By 1855 his debts from gambling were believed to have been £16,000, an eye watering £2.25 million in today's money. The last straw was when his horse, Nettle, bought at Belleisle, came undone in the 1855 Oaks. Nettle was one of the favourites for the race, with a chance of winning the £10,000 prize. Instead it bolted and fell over the chain near the new mile post, breaking the jockey, Marlow's, leg. The horse was later to be re-named Vengeance and ran second at the Cesarewitch.

John Parsons Cook, by comparison, had more success with his horses and won the Shrewsbury Cup, with a prize of £2,400. In a fit of jealousy, Palmer now plotted to murder his friend. After a day at Shrewsbury races, where Palmer had lost heavily, he had dinner with Cook and four friends at the Raven Inn near Shrewsbury. Shortly afterwards, Cook became ill, but to Palmer's frustration he recovered. A few days later Palmer met Cook for a drink and administered three grains of strychnine in Cook's drink. Cook died an agonising death on 21 November 1855. *The Illustrated Times*, reporting on the trial, described Cook: *'Wildly shrieking, the patient tossed about in fearful convulsions; his limbs were so rigid that it was impossible to raise him, though he entreated that they would do so, as he felt that he was suffocating.'* Palmer then interfered with the post mortem, carried out by a medical student, by taking away the stomach contents. He even sent a letter to the coroner, asking for a verdict of accidental death and enclosing a £10 note.

To no avail. Palmer was arrested. What followed was a sensational trial, which began on 14 May 1856. It even made legal history as it required an Act of Parliament to allow the trial to be held at the Old Bailey. The trial was hugely controversial, with claim and counter-claim, and Palmer professing his innocence to the last. Palmer, then aged 31, was found guilty and executed by public hanging outside Stafford Gaol on 14 June 1856. So notorious had the case become that his death attracted a crowd of 35,000, many of them shouting 'poisoner'.

Courtroom Scene from the Trial of William Palmer

William Palmer became known as the 'Prince of Poisoners'. Charles Dickens called him 'the greatest villain that stood at the Old Bailey'. At his trial,

Palmer was charged and found guilty of the wilful murder of three persons. Eventually, a total of fourteen deaths were attributed to his actions, including his friend, Cook, his mother-in-law, four of his five children, his wife Annie and his brother, Walter. The case became even more notorious because it was the first case in British criminal history where strychnine was used for the purposes of murder.

Palmer's notoriety lived on long after his death. His waxwork stood in Madame Tussaud's Chamber of Horrors for almost 130 years. In 1957 Robert Graves wrote a book covering the trial, entitled *They Hanged my Saintly Billy*. The BBC then made the story into a film in 1998, *The Life and Crimes of William Palmer*. So it was that, for all the wrong reasons, the name of Belleisle Stables, Richmond, became so well known.

Racing in 1868

By 1868 Richmond races and attendances had begun to decline through a variety of factors. Horse racing nationally remained popular but its centre of gravity was now in the south and midlands, not in the north. Many Yorkshire landowners and their families found London life increasingly attractive and spent less time on their estates. Ever-increasing numbers of owners lived in the south. First the coach routes and then the rail routes increasingly by-passed Richmond. Horses no longer had to be walked to meetings over several days but could now travel rapidly by rail. From the 1850s onwards some racecourses near to large centres of population relied less on local collections and subscriptions, enclosing the course instead and charging entrance fees to the large crowds that attended. At the same time, the carnival atmosphere of the race meeting, its noise, gambling and drinking, and occasional drunken fights, were attracting increased opposition from the more respectable and religious of the middle and upper classes. The evenings after the races created a more unacceptable disturbance for many than previously. Richmond now had only a two-day meeting, on 15 and 16 September. The horses were mainly locally trained and of a low standard, with more handicap and short-distance races for inexperienced horses. The Richmond branch of the North Eastern Railway brought visitors from Newcastle, Sunderland and Durham, as well as Leeds, but local interest was lessening and crowds were small on both days, although there were still family parties, luncheons and picnics on the course. Urban gate-money meetings could endow rich stakes, but the thinly populated region around Richmond could only raise relatively small amounts for prize money through its town collection, though the local MPs and Earl of Zetland still gave financial support. Good horses were sent elsewhere. Ever larger numbers of professional gamblers, pickpockets and tricksters were now arriving by train and exploiting the more naïve locals and country people, which increased the cost of paying the county police and specialist racing detectives and angered local magistrates and the Corporation.

Final decline

From 1870 onwards the Jockey Club began to introduce new rules which bore down on small country meetings like Richmond's, pushing for increased prize money and safer courses. By 1890 there were 190 rules of racing, which Richmond struggled to meet. The racing press began to describe Richmond as on old-fashioned meeting. Despite the hard work of the local race committee, generous donations from the local MP and the Earl of Zetland, and the support of the Zetland family, who usually brought up a party for the races, fewer local inhabitants took an interest in it, and race meetings were now often poorly attended. The two-day race meeting gained little praise in the racing press, described as tame and uninteresting, or as a poor day's racing. Reports stressed the presence of card sharps, drunkards and pickpockets. Deficits in the accounts began to appear more regularly, and it became increasingly difficult to hold a two-day meeting. Long-time committee members such as John Wetherell, the Richmond auctioneer, and Alderman Alexander Young, brewer, wine and spirit merchant and racehorse breeder, were dying off. The race committee decided to enclose the course and charge admission, but, despite charging a shilling for entrance in 1889, a year when the local vicar preached against the meeting, the following year only £200 was taken at the turnstiles and £225 at the Grandstand, suggesting attendances of perhaps 3,000 or so, while the meeting cost over £1,000 to run. The Earl of Zetland provided £200 towards the meeting in 1892, but the whole town only subscribed £62. Finances were bad and, in addition, the Jockey Club required course alterations and improvements to safety which could not be afforded. Closure was inevitable and the final meeting was held on 7 August 1891.

Early photo of the Grandstand from around 1860

FROM - A VISIT TO RICHMOND PHOTOGRAPHS FROM THE 1860'S BY AUDREY CARR

Part 2
THE RACECOURSE SINCE 1892 AND THE FIGHT TO SAVE THE GRANDSTAND

With the end of public race meetings in 1891, the buildings on the racecourse were now no longer necessary for the roles that they were designed to perform. The grandstand, which had been paid for by public subscription, and the judge's box (referred to as the 'Stewards' Stand') were now put up for sale. What emerges from the records of the time regarding the sales, however, leaves several questions unanswered!

On 12 June 1897 the Borough Council, despite claiming since the time of the 1853 Act (to be explained in Part 4) that it owned the grandstand, paid £50 (£6,500 at today's prices) to take possession of the building. The Richmond Borough Houses and Building Committee reported that it had paid the sum that day to a body entitled 'The Proprietors of the Grandstand'. Receipt of £50 was acknowledged by Thos. Carter in his capacity as 'Chairman [the word is a little indistinct in the records] of the Committee of Proprietors of the Grandstand'. In return, Carter handed over 'the key and possession of the Grandstand in full settlement of all claims by them, except for the rights of holders of medals of admission to the Stand to admission at any race meetings to be held on Richmond Race Course'. (There were, of course, to be no future race meetings).

Thomas Carter was Deputy Chairman of the Burgage Pastures Committee between 1892 and 1897, which includes the year of the sale, before becoming Chairman in 1908. He was a doctor, a local magistrate and physician to various local institutions such as the workhouse. He was also Warden of the Mercers, Grocers and Haberdashers, the most senior of Richmond's companies of merchants and craftsmen. The Burgage Pastures minute books, however, fail to cast any light on the origin or status of the 'Proprietors of the Grandstand', of whose Committee Carter was the Chairman. Nor do the Burgage Pastures account books show any evidence that £50 was ever received by them. Professor Huggins has commented that Carter's name crops up regularly as a member of committees associated with the racecourse and it was possible that, at the time of the sale, he was acting on behalf of the families or estates of those who had paid for the building of the grandstand in 1776 by purchasing medals or tokens.

At the time of the sale, Richmond Borough Houses and Building Committee also agreed to continue a tenancy by the said Dr Carter on behalf of the 4th Battalion Yorkshire Regiment until May Day 1898 and a payment of £5 for that period was received. As well as his many roles on the Burgage Pastures Committee and the Committee of the Proprietors of the Grandstand, Dr Carter was also physician to the local militia.

At a meeting held on 22 March 1898, the Borough Surveyor reported that, on the basis of his inspection, repairs needed to put the grandstand into a suitable state externally and internally would cost £92. It was also recorded that the building was currently let up to 13 May (the May Day letting agreed with Carter) and recommended that it be advertised for hire for future camping-ground purposes. This would have referred to its use as an army camping-ground as described in Part 3 of this book.

Next came the sale of the 'Stewards' Stand' in 1898. The Borough Council Coucher Book records include an observation by the Houses and Building Committee that the 'Stewards or smaller stand … adjoining the one belonging to the Corporation … was advertised for sale by public auction on Saturday 26th March (1898) and recommended that the advisability of the Council buying the stand be taken into consideration'.

The *Sporting Life* of 28 March 1898 reported that: 'The Stewards Stand on Richmond Racecourse was on Saturday (26th March) sold by public auction at the King's Head Hotel by John Weatherall [sic].' The original price (it was said) was £300 and it was sold to Councillor S.W. Close representing the Richmond Corporation for £30. (S.W. Close was one of the Councillors listed in the record of the sale of the grandstand).

This notice of sale is very unclear as to which building it refers to. The stand being sold is described as being 'adjoining the one belonging to the Corporation' and the term used is the 'Stewards Stand' rather than the judge's box. The sale only makes sense, however, if it refers to the judge's box. The Zetland Stand remained as private property and was never in the possession of the Corporation. This was made clear in 1969/70 by the North Riding County Planning Committee when the Borough applied for permission to demolish the grandstand, the Zetland Stand and the judge's box on health and safety grounds (a story described later in this book). The Borough subsequently wrote to Lord Zetland concerning the condition of his stand.

Other uses of the racecourse and the grandstand after 1892

In addition to its use as a site for annual military training camps, recorded at the time of the sale of the grandstand in 1897, Richmond Racecourse and grandstand have seen a wide variety of other uses.

The location of the racecourse and its wide open spaces made it an ideal venue for an eclectic range of other outdoor sporting activities such as golf. Richmond Golf Club was established in 1892, with play taking place on the racecourse site. The *Leeds and Mercury Post* reported on the half-yearly golf competition for the Silver Bowl in November 1901, played out on the racecourse links, which was presented to the winner by the Commander of the Princess of Wales' Own Regiment. The *Sunderland Echo* reported a story of a woman who could not get her son to go to school because he was earning plenty of money as a caddy for various gentlemen playing golf on Richmond Racecourse. Her complaint seemed to be as much that he refused to give her any of the money, claiming to have spent it on cigarettes and the like! The use of the racecourse as a golf course came to an end in 1904. The *Leeds Intelligencer* of 24 September reported that the town had laid out a new golf course because the long grass on the racecourse made playing golf an impossibility during the spring and summer months.

The racecourse was a regular meeting place for the Zetland Hunt. The *Whitby Gazette* of April 1911 reported that the Marquess's last season as Master of Hounds had been attended with much success on the old racecourse, with the Marchioness following the hounds to their first draw in her car. An account of April 1914 describes how some 70 followers of the Zetland pack, with Mr Gilbert Straker at the head, met before the grandstand in a vigorous south-westerly wind, before enjoying good sport. In 1905 the racecourse had also been used for pigeon shooting, with sweepstakes promoted by Richmond gunsmith, Mr Metcalf.

An event that took place from time to time on the racecourse site was the competition for the Scorton Arrow. This ancient archery competition, held annually by the Society of Archers, goes back to 1673. The winner of the silver arrow is the first archer to pierce a three-inch diameter black spot, placed inside a four-foot target, over a distance of 100 yards. The winner each year then nominates the venue for the following year, though by its rules it can only be shot for in Yorkshire and Teesside. The competition has been held in Richmond 79 times since it began, some of which have been on the racecourse site. Fairfax-Blakeborough records that: 'The Scorton Arrow was competed for at Richmond Racecourse on Wednesday 27th June 1815 and gentlemen who intended to shoot were requested to meet at the Golden Fleece Inn Richmond at nine in the forenoon'.

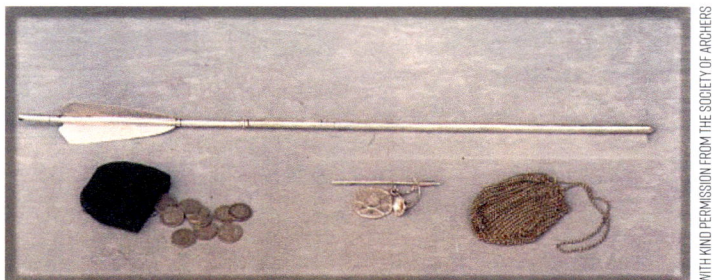

Scorton Silver Arrow

Although commercial racing had now come to a close, the racetrack and its wide open spaces were still an ideal area for exercising and training horses with the permission of the Burgage Pastures Committee, which owned the right to use the land.

Grandstand illustration regularly reproduced

On occasion, trainers and owners used the racecourse to exercise their horses without the permission of the Burgage Pastures Committee. In February 1925 a case came before the County Court judge in Darlington as to the right to use the Richmond training grounds without permission. The Burgage Pastures Committee claimed £15 from James Peacock for training some 'flappers' (horses not recognised by the Jockey Club) and causing damage to the gallops. It also sought an injunction to prohibit the defendant from further trespass on the historic training grounds. The judge found for the Burgage Pastures Committee, but, because there was no evidence of what damage had been caused, said that he could not award more than £1 in damages, although the injunction on unauthorised use of the racecourse was approved.

Formal race meetings on the racecourse may have ended, but the Burgage Pastures Committee continued to levy galloping fees, rents and eatage to the surrounding racing stables, which made regular legitimate use of the racecourse. Private galloping matches still took place from time to time. The *York Herald* on 14 August 1900 reported that a galloping match over one mile took place on Richmond racecourse between Wheel of Fortune, belonging to the son of Richmond's Mayor, and Adam Fawcett's Miss Nellie.

Richmond and its racecourse continued to be a major racehorse training and breeding centre for many years after 1892.

A short account of the racing stables in and around Richmond

In February 1875 a racing correspondent wrote in the *York Herald:* 'For more than a century and a half, the fine old borough of Richmond has maintained its reputation as one of the principal places in Yorkshire for the breeding, training and racing of the British Thoroughbred. Four breeding studs are kept within the sound of Richmond's bells and there are 4 or 5 racing stables around the town. Mr Blenkiron has a stallion or two and a few breeding mares in the grounds attached to the old ruin of Easby Abbey. Weatherbit was a famous stallion that occupied the box of Emilius at Easby, the last Derby that Frank Buckle rode to victory. Emilius now lies buried in a paddock under the shadow of an ivy crowned wing of the ruin [of the abbey], the soundest portions of which have, for many years, acted as boxes for brood mares and their sucklings. The town of Richmond is literally full of turf reminiscences, and a tradesman of the place who could not 'talk horse' might as well pull down his sign and shove up his shutters.'

'I could not name a place in England where an old sportsman, whose health requires a stimulant from the reinvigorating air of the country, could not pass a few weeks more cheerily than a daily walk down to the training grounds of Richmond. He would first pass Silvio House and training stables on Hurgill Road, so called after the racehorse who once won the Gold Cup on the moor. On ascending the hill for only a short distance further, he could not fail to notice the training establishment at Belleisle. Arriving at the crest of the hill, he will probably notice a troop of brood mares nibbling with a dainty bite on the sweet herbage that grows on the rich limestone of which these grand old hills are formed. These are part of the stud of High Gingerfield, owned by Mr Wright. The stables were first used by Charles and John Writtingham, who trained many a good horse. Boxes snug and well ventilated, and the land is excellent ... within easy reach of the High Moor, where the going is always good, and the racecourse.'

Sadly, Richmond's racing stables have now all disappeared, but their names and the memory of their horses and trainers live on.

Silvio House, situated in Hurgill Road, was one such notable racing stable. It was named after a famous horse called Silvio, owned by a Mr Hutton, who came second in the Richmond Gold Cup on four occasions, before winning it in 1764. Charles Dawson, the horse's jockey, became a trainer to Sir Lawrence Dundas at Silvio House, which subsequently became a public stable.

The first information on Temple View Stables is about George Kennedy in *Northern Turf History* having built stables there in the 1860s, run by Thomas Lunn. Thomas had gone to Belleisle at the age of ten as an apprentice to John Gill. After working at Middleham, he returned to Richmond in the 1860s to the Temple View Stables, with the Mastermans as his main patrons. The success of the horses owned by the confederacy soon brought additional patrons and many more horses. Having known Richmond in its heyday as a centre of training and as a popular race meeting, Thomas lived to see racing come to an end in 1891 and the subsequent decline of training at

Temple View, until he had only two horses left. He died of pneumonia in 1909.

This was not quite the end of the Temple View Stables, however. The *Leeds Mercury*, on Wednesday 14 January 1925, reported on the career of Major Willie Renwick who left his father's shipping business to join his brother Jack as a trainer in Malton, before moving to the Temple View Stables. Here, he kept and trained a relatively small string of horses, though with some success. During 1924, the stable won nine races, to a value of £1,713, on the flat, and nine races, to a value of £850, under National Hunt Rules. Each autumn, yearlings from the stud of his father, Sir George Renwick, at Newminster Abbey, Morpeth, would be sent to Richmond for training.

In 1925, there were sixteen horses at Temple View, with five vacant boxes. In 1928 Willie Renwick schooled a horse called Trump Card, a favourite for the Grand National, over fences on the old Richmond racecourse. Unfortunately for the stable, however, the 1928 Grand National was to prove a unique event. Due in part to the misty, wet weather and heavy going, only two of the runners finished the race, a record in Grand National history. Trump Card was one of the fallers. Renwick's son, Aubrey, took out a licence, but only trained for a couple of seasons before taking up a position with the *Sporting Life*. In 1932, we learn that a Mr Renton, who trained a big team of horses at Oxclose, Ripon, took on Temple View Stables to use in addition to his Ripon stables.

Easby Stud was owned by the Jaques family of Easby Hall. When Robert Jaques, a breeder of horses, bought Easby Hall in 1814, he turned the property into a breeding stud, which included the site of Easby Abbey, as well as the Hall itself. His son, Richard,

Sam Bone supervising exercise of the stable's horses on the racecourse

wrote a book about the stud in 1860 and its many famous racing horses, such as Emilius, winner of the Derby, who came to Easby for the last years of his stud career before dying and being buried in the Abbey grounds.

The report in the *York Herald* of February 1875 on High Gingerfield Lodge includes a description of the stud groom, Sam Bone, who was typical of the stables in those days, dressed in breeches and gaiters, cravat and well-worn silk hat.

Belleisle, situated adjacent to Richmond racecourse, was one of the most successful training establishments in the town. The first incumbent was Billy Peirse, who became a successful jockey, trainer and owner. His horses won the St Leger in 1817 and 1818. On the latter occasion he owned and trained the first two horses and also trained the horse in third place. His son, Tom, was followed by the Gill brothers, John and Edward. First, John took over in 1835 and worked with Lord Zetland's famous horse, Voltigeur (whose part in the 'Match of the Century' against The Flying Dutchman in 1851 is told elsewhere in this book). John was succeeded by his brother, Edward, who maintained that the high point of his career was the sale of the two racehorses, Chicken and Nettle, to the 'Prince of Poisoners', Dr William Palmer, in 1854 in the parlour at Belleisle. (This story is also told elsewhere in this book).

James Watson followed on from the Gills at Belleisle for 40 years, winning many races including the Northumberland Plate.

Another famous trainer associated with Richmond was Harry Peacock, son of the famous Middleham trainer, Dobson Peacock. Lawrence Dundas, 2nd Marquess of Zetland, in his memoirs *Racing: a Hereditary Pastime*, described how his horses had been trained on the Richmond Low Moor, the site of the old racecourse, after the retirement of his brother, George. For some little time he had thought of building a house and stables suitable for a training establishment close to both the Low Moor and the High Moor. This became the Hurgill Lodge Stables, into which Harry Peacock moved on 14 January 1937. That same year, Harry Peacock's horse, Marmaduke Jinks, won the Lincolnshire Handicap, which was not only a good beginning for the stables but once more put Richmond on the map as a training centre. He then moved his brood mares into Belleisle in 1938. (Marmaduke Jinks is one of the horses in the board game Totopoly, the racing version of Monopoly.)

At this time Harry had 53 horses in training at Hurgill Lodge, all of them transported to races by the British Railways motor horse box service.

Lord Zetland with Racehorse Trainer Harry Peacock

Harry Peacock trained many famous horses on the racecourse gallops, one of which was the 1954 early Derby favourite, Rowston Moor. An article by the racing correspondent 'Gimcrack' described how the tight bends of the old racecourse track, especially its Tattenham Corner, were an ideal preparation for the biggest colt in the Derby to learn how to run fast round sharp left-hand corners. Unfortunately, the training did not bring success in the actual race, which was won by a young Lester Piggott on the American colt, Never Say Die.

Buster Fenningworth with his dog Jet in 1964. The Grandstand and the Zetland Stand, although not in 'tip top' condition, were still substantially intact

When he retired in 1961, Harry Peacock was succeeded by his son-in-law, George 'Buster' Fenningworth. Rarely seen on course without his good luck charm – a battered trilby hat – Fenningworth boasted the largest string in the north by 1966, with 80 horses in his care. Among his owners were the Marquess of Zetland, Lady Sassoon, and the film star, James Stewart. Buster enjoyed his best season in 1962, training 52 winners, including Bordonne, who beat the Queen's horse, Optimistic, by a short head in the Northumberland Plate.

Sadly, Buster died in a car accident in April 1967, on his way to a race meeting in Ayr.

An equally eminent trainer at Hurgill Lodge was Bill Watts, who took up the mantle with great success in 1970. Watts trained Waterloo, the winner of the 1,000 Guineas, on the old racecourse and also trained Teleprompter, winner of the Arlington Million in America, so named because it carried a winning purse of a million dollars.

Some of the stables were to be found in the very heart of Richmond. There was a stable in Queen's Road on the site that is currently occupied by Calverts Carpets. Yet another was the Green Stables, a small establishment at the Old Brewery on the Green, associated with Charles Kennedy. The *Leeds Mercury* of 25 January 1925 describes the Green Stables as once being important, but by that time it had become non-existent, with Temple View Stables holding sway.

Come wind, come hail, come snow… the local stables exercised their horses on Low Moor

The total eclipse of the sun, 1927

The position of the racecourse also saw it used for some memorable events that were not connected with racehorses.

On 29 June 1927 Richmond became the 'hub of the Eclipse universe' (from the *Northern Echo* headline), as thousands of people came by road and rail to witness the total eclipse of the sun. The town was considered to be the best place to view this rare event, the first time it had happened in central Britain for 200 years, because it lay on the centre line of totality. The racecourse, set high above the town, was where most of the vast crowd gathered on that memorable morning.

So many trains came from London that passengers had to disembark at Broken Brea level crossing, just outside Richmond. There was simply not enough platform space at the station to cope with the hordes of people who descended on the town. Astronomers from all over the world even came to Richmond Racecourse to set up their telescopes.

A fourteen-year-old Richmond boy, Leslie Thorpe, recounted in his diary how everyone had a wonderful time. He described how street traders were out in force, selling pieces of smoked glass and goggles and anything else they could make a few coppers on. There were even amusements in the Market Place for the occasion. A Grand Ball was held in the Castle Grounds, with what the social calendar for that week described as 'electricity effects' to enhance the occasion.

Then, around 4 a.m., the crowds set off up Hurgill Road towards the Low Moor to witness the spectacle of the eclipse.

It hardly mattered that the cloud level frustrated the actual sighting of the eclipse. Leslie wrote that '...when it came, it was very eerie. From brilliant sunshine everything went grey, then black ... pitch black. The dogs started barking and the kiddies crying'. Grandfather Parkyn, in his account of the eclipse, describes how '... the grass and objects became strange, with a violet colour hue; even the

One of Richmond's popular landmarks, located in Victoria Road, commemorates the 1927 Solar Eclipse

cattle and farm stock, which, a few minutes earlier, had been carrying on their usual bleat, now became very quiet'.

Virginia Woolf and other members of the Bloomsbury Set, Vita Sackville-West, Harold Nicholson and Quentin Bell, were among those who made the journey to Richmond from London. Woolf wrote a description of the event in her diary. The extract is entitled *A Moment's Liberty*.

Portrait of Virginia Woolf – 1902 by George Charles Beresford

'Left by train 10 pm on one of the Eclipse specials from ... Kings Cross. It was a five and a half hour ride to Richmond in North Yorkshire. It was impossible to sleep on the train, so I passed the time smoking cigars. We got to Richmond about 3.30 am.... then here was a level crossing, at which were drawn up a long line of motor omnibuses and motors ... As we crept up to the top of the moor there were people sleeping in their cars ... people had already taken up positions. So we joined them, walking out to what seemed the highest point looking over Richmond... We could see by a gold spot where the sun was. We began to get anxious and saw rays coming through the bottom of the clouds ... We got out our smoked glasses ... We saw the sun, we saw it crescent, burning red. The next moment it had sailed fast into the cloud again. The moments were passing. We thought we were cheated. .. But now the colour was going out. Clouds turning a reddish black. The 24 seconds were passing. [The eclipse actually lasted 23 seconds] Then... very, quickly, it became darker and darker... when, suddenly, the light went out. There was no colour.

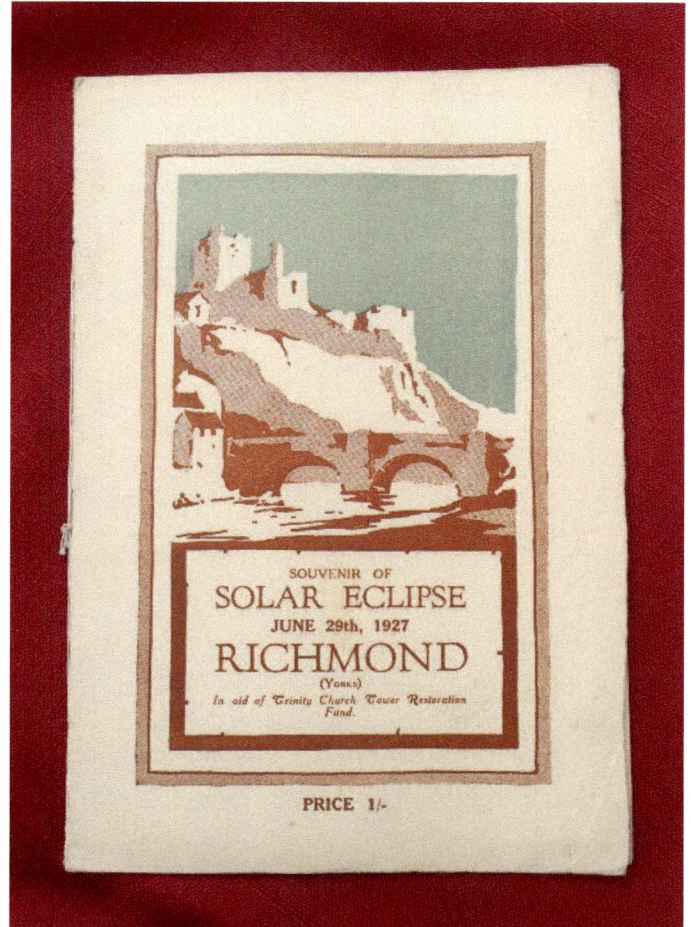

Souvenir programme for the 1927 Solar Eclipse

The earth was dead... the next [moment] the cloud took colour on itself again; and so the light came back. The colour for some moments was as the most lovely kind– fresh, various – here blue and there brown ... all new colours, as if washed over and repainted. Then it was over...'

It is estimated that some 30,000 people viewed the eclipse at Richmond, most of them from the racecourse ('by kind permission of the Burgage Owners Committee. Admission 6d.'). The event raised significant funds for the town, with the money being used to restore Trinity Tower, which was in danger of collapsing after the surrounding shops had been demolished.

The isolation hospital on the racecourse

One of the last uses that the grandstand was put to was as an isolation hospital.

Before the establishment of the Ministry of Health in 1919, public health measures were taken at a local level. The Infectious Diseases (Notification) Act 1889 made it compulsory to notify local medical officers of health of any infectious diseases and to compel sufferers to be sent to an isolation hospital. The Isolation Hospitals Acts 1893-1901 then empowered county and county borough councils to promote the establishment of hospitals for infectious diseases in districts where there was an apparent need.

In the winter of 1901–2, the last major smallpox epidemic in England broke out in London. The disease spread northward and Richmond acted accordingly. Because it was thought too dangerous for patients to be sent to the existing isolation hospital, the Borough Council (also still known as the Corporation) decided to use the racecourse grandstand instead. On 21 March 1902, the *Yorkshire Evening Post* reported that the grandstand had been rented by the Corporation Sanitary Committee.

Fortunately, the smallpox outbreak had died away by 1904. There were few further cases of smallpox in Richmond after this time, although in June 1925 the *Leeds Intelligencer* reported that Medical Officer Dr John Williams had informed the Richmond Rural Council that a case of smallpox had been discovered in the HH Lines at Catterick Garrison. The patient had been removed to the hospital on Richmond racecourse.

Smallpox was not the only infectious disease that the isolation hospital in the grandstand was used for. Some time prior to the Great War of 1914-18 there was an outbreak of typhoid in Richmond and the grandstand was once again used as an isolation area. A lady called Mrs Armstrong, who was an auxiliary nurse at the Victoria Hospital at the time, was put in charge. With no contact allowed, food, letters and papers and other necessities were carried up Hurgill Road and left opposite the grandstand by Mr John Willie Bolland (Mrs Armstrong's brother-in-law) and other men, who would shout out messages to Mrs Armstrong and the patients isolated there.

The Richmond Borough Executive Committee Minutes provide an insight into the level of care that was taken in maintaining the building as an isolation hospital during this period. The fireplace in the grandstand was repaired in 1913 at a cost 'not exceeding £1', and the building was thoroughly cleaned every year. In 1923 there is a reference to the rooms at the grandstand being 'colour washed and cleaned', and in 1925 the Borough Surveyor ordered that 'the Grandstand roof be repaired and fires lighted in the building twice a week'. In 1926 it was decided that 'the iron bedsteads be re-lacquered'.

There were, however, some setbacks in the maintenance of the building. The *Yorkshire Post* on 26 September 1930 reported that: ' A fire broke out yesterday in the Grandstand on Richmond Racecourse, about a mile from the town, which is used as an Isolation Hospital, but is at present unoccupied …. A corporation workman gave the alarm. Alderman M. Mason and the Borough Surveyor, Mr H. Kendall, motored to the Grandstand with fire extinguishers. Beams had to be cut away before the fire could be quelled. The flooring, the ceiling of one ward and two beds and mattresses were destroyed'.

The commitment by the Borough to maintain the building as an isolation hospital lasted until 1941, when agreement was reached with Middlesbrough Town Council that future cases would be treated there.

The military made regular use of the racecourse, the grandstand and the surrounding site throughout the twentieth century. Its use as a camping and training area had actually begun before racing ceased in 1891 and it was not until the early 1960s that the Gallowgate Camp, on the site adjacent to the racecourse, was closed down, having been declared surplus to military requirements by the War Department. This strong military tradition forms part of the history of Richmond and its racecourse; the story is told separately in Part 3 *The military on the racecourse.*

The grandstand's sad decline

The use of the site and its buildings during WW2 brought additional concerns about the maintenance of the grandstand. By September 1941 the Borough Finance Committee was concerned about the condition of the grandstand and it was formally inspected by the Town Clerk and the Borough Surveyor. (Richmond had become a Municipal Borough under the Municipal Corporations Act of 1835. The title of 'Borough' remained in use until the Local Government reorganisation in 1974. Despite this, the term 'Town Clerk' was still used for the Borough Council's official).

The Town Clerk and Borough Surveyor reported 'a great deal of wanton damage … both to the fabric of the building and the iron railings which surround it'. It was reported that the Town Clerk was 'taking up with the Military Authorities and others, the question of placing the Old Grandstand and the Old Judge's Stand out of bounds, in order that, in due course, the Corporation can take suitable steps for the preservation of these unique buildings' (North Yorkshire County Records Office). We have no corroborative evidence that this took place.

The need for war materials placed a burden on the fabric of the building. It was recommended that, 'except for the several iron gate entrances', all the

Aerial photograph of the Grandstands in their current state of disrepair

railings around the grandstand be removed and passed over to the Borough Surveyor, who was responsible locally for the campaign to salvage ironwork for re-use as munitions. The *Yorkshire Post*, in September 1941, reported that the railings were subsequently removed and made available for salvage.

Attitudes regarding the preservation of the buildings seem to have changed immediately after the end of the War, however, when the Borough Council decided to remove the lead from the roof in order to sell it. Thieves had already taken illegal action to remove the grandstand lead in 1948. Two persons were apprehended, convicted and fined. A further culprit in 1950 was convicted and ordered to repay the £20 cost of the damage at 10s per week. Then in 1951 the Borough Corporation itself removed the sheet lead from the roof, intending to sell it to the Water Department.

Despite the degradation of their fabric, the historical importance of the racecourse buildings was beginning to be recognised at a national level. In 1952 the grandstand was included in the first statutory list of buildings of special architectural and historic interest and was listed Grade II. Also included were the judge's box and Moor Cottage (the former West Lodge, now known as High Lodge). In 1988 the grandstand was raised to Grade II*, putting the remains among the top 6% of listed buildings in the country.

Partial demolition of the grandstand

The period 1969–70 saw a conflict over the Borough Council's concern about health and safety issues associated with the decaying buildings on the racecourse and the North Riding County Council's desire to safeguard the architectural heritage of the buildings. The outcome was a contentious partial demolition of the grandstand by the Borough Council.

The Borough's intentions had already been shown in September 1959, when the Council gave notice to the Ministry of Housing and Local Government of its intention to demolish the grandstand. Tenders were advertised for demolition, the purchase of the stone and the clearance of the site. Then, at a meeting held in January 1960, the Borough Council decided not to proceed at this stage. This was to prove only a temporary reprieve.

In January 1969 Richmond Borough Council applied to the North Riding County Council to demolish the grandstand (application 643/LB) and the judge's box (application 644/LB) on the grounds that they were unsafe for children playing in the structures. The 1968 Town and Country Planning Act allowed the Borough Council to take action if the structure of the buildings were deemed to be a hazard to the public. The Borough's own actions in removing the lead from the roofs of the buildings some years earlier had, of course, done much to contribute to their decayed condition.

The County Planning Sub-Committee first visited the site (the picture of this visit is shown below) before a meeting in which the Committee refused the Borough's applications. It did so on the grounds that each building was a 'Grade II building included in the List of Buildings of Architectural or Historical Interest'. It also said that each of the buildings was 'of considerable interest in its representation of the history of the locality'. In addition, it removed what it referred to as the Old Stand (meaning the Zetland Stand adjacent to the main grandstand)

Site meeting of the North Riding Planning Committee, 8th July 1969... "which Richmond Borough Council was keen to pull down

from the application as it was not owned by the Borough. It stated: 'In point of fact the Borough Council's application was amended to exclude the Old Stand as this was not in their ownership and refusal therefore was to the amended application to demolish the larger Grandstand and the Old Judges Box'.

On receipt of the County's letter of refusal, Richmond Borough Council asked the County to undertake to relieve the Borough of all future responsibility for accidents and to pay towards a substantial fence. The most that the County offered was an *ex gratia* payment towards additional insurance premiums payable by the Corporation because of the increased risk.

In November 1969, the Borough decided, under the powers granted by the 1968 Act, to appeal to the Ministry of Housing and Local Government against the County's refusal to authorise demolition. The Ministry's response to the appeal was discussed at a meeting of the Borough General Purposes Committee held on 13 January 1970. The Borough was authorised by the Ministry to obtain a report from an independent architect as to the condition of the grandstand and as to possible means of making the structure safe. The firm of Sanderson, Townend and Gilbert was duly commissioned to carry out the inspection.

The General Purposes Committee discussed the firm's report at a meeting held in March 1970. It was then resolved to serve a Notice on the County under Section 40(8) of the 1968 Act indicating that the Borough intended to render the grandstand safe as soon as possible by removing the top storey of the building, so reducing its height to 12 feet, and to remove the three remaining pillars at the front of the building. The material would be deposited inside the remainder of the building.

On receipt of the surveyor's report and the Borough's Notice of Intent, the North Riding Planning Committee felt obliged to end its resistance to the partial demolition, albeit with great reluctance. The County Council minutes for April 1970 record the Planning Committee's report: 'The Borough Council have since informed your [Planning] Committee of their great concerns about the condition of the Old Grandstand and possible injury to persons. The Borough Council have stated that the structure is in danger of collapsing and their statement is supported by a surveyor's report. In the circumstances, your [Planning] Committee have accepted the Borough Council's view ... and have said that the County Council as local planning authority will take no action if this is done'. Clearly, the North Riding Planning Committee still felt unable to approve the destruction of a building 'included in the Statutory list of Buildings of Architectural or Historical Interest', but now felt unable to prevent this act of corporate vandalism.

On 14 April 1970, the Town Clerk reported to the General Purposes Committee that the County had 'in effect' acquiesced to the proposal. Tenders for the work were submitted by the Borough Surveyor and it was agreed to accept the lowest tender received, namely that for £216 from Blairs of Darlington. The partial demolition began soon afterwards, in June 1970.

The partial demolition was permitted and carried out only on the main grandstand building. Accordingly, the Borough proposed 'that a copy of the report be forwarded to Lord Zetland and his attention drawn to the observations made on the building known as Lord Zetland's Box so that he might consider taking any appropriate action in the light of the Council's proposals for the Grandstand'.

This did not end the controversy. When the Borough attempted to remove the demolished stone from the site in order to sell it and defray its costs, Lord Zetland and the Burgage Pastures Committee, beginning their campaign to preserve Richmond's racing heritage, refused consent for it to be carted away and locked the gate.

So it was that the grandstand was reduced to its present, sad, state.

The famous author of many books on the history of horse racing, Fairfax-Blakeborough, commented that 'when the grandstand was derequisitioned by the Air Force [at the end of WW2], it was left in perfect condition but it had been allowed to fall into disrepair by the town authority as no other building with such a rich heritage of memories would have been… Many far removed from the Richmond area will feel grieved at a sad and shameful demolition of a visible link with the historic sporting past'.

Architectural historian, Jane Hatcher, wrote in her 1990 book *Richmondshire Architecture* that, 'Where there had been a Georgian building of outstanding quality, there was now a pathetic relic, deliberately smashed by the hand of bungling bureaucracy'.

In 1974, as part of Local Government reorganisation, Richmond Borough Council was replaced by Richmondshire District Council. As part of the reorganisation, the District Council assumed ownership of the historic racecourse buildings. The new authority began to show a different attitude regarding their preservation from that of the old Borough Council.

By 1985 Richmondshire District Council had started a concerted effort to find a new use for the grandstand which could lead to its restoration. Under the Chief Planning Officer, Bill Green, the District Council Technical Department even prepared plans showing how to reconstruct the grandstand. It was suggested that approaches be made to the Landmark Trust (a British building conservation charity founded in 1965). Despite a considerable amount of initial interest, however, the Landmark Trust concluded in 1988 against involvement on the grounds that

Richmond Racecourse – Aerial view looking east to west

the grandstand was too large and too degraded for the Trust to undertake to save it. Other potential buildings were more complete. The Landmark Trust was asked to consider the project again in 1999, but reached the same conclusion.

English Heritage, set up in 1983 as the Historic Buildings and Monuments Commission, was also contacted in 1986 and the grandstand was assessed as clearly having been outstanding when it was complete and 'one of Richmond's finest Georgian buildings,' as well as 'one of the earliest known racecourse grandstands in the country'. It was at this point, in 1988, that the status of the grandstand was raised to Grade II*. English Heritage offered a 'substantial sum' (reported in the *Weekend Telegraph* in October 1991 as £300,000) towards reconstruction, and offered grants under their new Building at Risk programme for an archaeological-type examination of the site to investigate how much original material remained. All that happened was that, in the autumn of 1989, a local building contractor was appointed to 'excavate' the grandstand, to sort and stack the stonework and bricks etc., and clear some of the brambles.

Efforts to involve the Vivat Trust (a charity set up to offer holiday lets in historical buildings) in a plan to re-purpose the grandstand as a holiday let were also pursued. In September 1991, the Vivat Trust launched an appeal and, in 1992, informed the Pasture Master that a distinguished York architect, Martin Sutcliffe, had been commissioned to undertake a feasibility study. Laura Norris of the Vivat Trust suggested the creation of a single-storey viewing platform from the grandstand. The Vivat Trust did not, however, proceed. Interestingly, at the annual meeting of the Burgage Pastures Committee in March 1995, Lord Zetland had reported that, at one stage, the Vivat Trust had suggested removing the grandstand from the racecourse and rebuilding it at Newmarket! The idea was never pursued. Jane Hatcher recalls that it was during the discussions with the Vivat Trust that Lord Zetland said he was happy for them to include his stand in any proposals for the grandstand.

Talks with English Heritage were resumed. At a meeting of the Burgage Pastures Committee, held in March 2002, Mr David Elliott, Conservation Officer for the District Council, reported that he had contacted English Heritage in December 1999 and that the grandstand had been added to the Register of Buildings at Risk in May 2000. A firm of architects had been appointed to look at the building and a range of preservation options and associated costs drawn up. These options ranged from 'Do Nothing' to a full restoration. At the meeting, Mr Elliott reported that the District Council and English Heritage had discussed the options. A full restoration was estimated to cost between £1m and £1.25m but the financial resources of English Heritage were limited. The preferred option of the District Council was, therefore, to 'protect and preserve the grandstand to prevent deterioration and thereafter manage it as a ruined building with the perimeter fence restored'.

In 2002 English Heritage drew up a brief for a Conservation Plan, to cover not just the buildings, but also the racecourse as a whole. At a meeting of interested organisations in 2004 to discuss the completed report, it was recognised that the racecourse, which was designated a Conservation Area in August 2004, 'was of national significance'.

Community uses of the racecourse

As racehorse training declined, so community uses of the site have continued to grow.

July 2006 saw the first Kite Festival, organised by the Richmondshire Building Preservation Trust Committee, to raise funds for the preservation and restoration of the old station as a community centre. Susan Holden, one of the Events Committee, had seen the success of kite festivals elsewhere, such as in Sunderland, and the racecourse site offered the ideal venue in Richmond. The application to the Burgage Pastures Committee to use the site in this way was exactly suited to the Committee's aspiration of seeking out wider uses for the racecourse. The event was so successful, attracting large crowds and filling the skyline with a spectacular display of colour, that it was repeated in the summer of 2007. Not only did the festivals raise funds for the station project, they also made many more people aware of the existence of the historic racecourse site and its superb views.

Kite Festival 2005 held to raise funds for the restoration of The Station

In 2016, large crowds flocked to the racecourse for the public viewing of the lighting of the Beacon to commemorate the Queen's 90th birthday.

The Burgage Pastures Committee receives ownership of the racecourse and its buildings

By 2005, the Burgage Pastures Committee had come to the conclusion that 'there was little future for the Grandstand at present and it was thought unlikely that the District Council wished to retain ownership'. Negotiations began with the District Council, and so it was that in 2008 the mantle of ownership of the racecourse and its buildings, its subsoil and the woodland above the Gallowfields Trading Estate, was handed over by Richmondshire District Council to the Burgage Pastures Committee.

The racecourse along with its buildings and the Low Moor have, therefore, passed under the freehold and stewardship of the Burgage Pastures Committee. It is the Committee which has continued the campaign to preserve and promote the racecourse site for the benefit of the community to the present day.

In 2011 the Committee began by making various improvements to the main car park on Whashton Road, the car park at the High Lodge, and the footpaths and signs. This has allowed the racecourse to be opened up more as an amenity for recreational use, particularly by dog walkers. The Committee realised, however, that, if it wished to do more than simply maintain and make small improvements to the racecourse, additional actions should be taken.

Firstly, the Committee would need to work in partnership with an organisation such as the Landmark Trust, a nationally acclaimed heritage restoration charity which had successfully restored the Culloden Tower in Richmond some years previously, or, perhaps, the Richmondshire Building Preservation Trust, a local charity which had successfully converted the Victorian station building into an award-winning social enterprise. The rationale behind this thinking was based on the fact that the Burgage Pastures Committee was not confident that it possessed the requisite skills to undertake what would be an extremely ambitious restoration project.

Secondly, the Committee would need to apply for the somewhat restrictive 1853 Burgage Pastures Act, a Private Member's Bill which governed the Committee's operation, to be amended in certain ways in order to bring it up to date and so allow some freedom and flexibility for any future plans to undertake necessary maintenance and even restoration work on the grandstand.

To have a Private Member's Bill amended, no matter how small the amendment one seeks, is a complicated and expensive process. As early as December 2003, the Burgage Pastures Committee had begun to investigate the feasibility of such a process by establishing contact with a London firm of solicitors and Parliamentary Agents called Sharpe Pritchard.

It wasn't until 2017 that a draft Bill was prepared by this firm. The Richmond Burgage Pastures Bill (103396.1) was then put to the House of Lords, initially for consideration by a small committee for scrutiny and approval, before going before the Lords and then the Commons. Unfortunately, a number of unexpected hurdles arose that significantly delayed the normal smooth passage of such uncontroversial bills. With the delays came mounting costs and no guarantee of success. So it was that the Committee reluctantly decided to withdraw its application in late 2018.

The obstacles then increased! In 1965, the Commons Registration Act had been passed to allow local authorities to formally register common land in order to protect it from future development and to secure it for the public benefit. In response to this, Richmond Borough Council had suggested to the Burgage Pastures Committee that the Richmond Racecourse land be registered as a common under the terms of the Act, even though it was still being used to exercise racehorses from neighbouring stables. The registration of the racecourse as a common duly took place in 1968.

Unfortunately, partly due to the limited time available to file the registration, combined with a less than clear understanding of the law regarding land which had pre-existing buildings on it, the Burgage Pastures Committee discovered that when the racecourse was initially registered under common land legislation in 1968, the buildings were mistakenly included. Many such errors were made at the time and a mechanism to correct these mistakes was set out in the Commons Act 2006. In 2019, therefore, the Committee applied to 'correct a mistaken registration' with North Yorkshire County Council, which determines the validity of such requests. The application was to 'de-register' the 'physical structures' on the course (namely, the grandstand, the judge's box and the Zetland Stand) which were wrongly registered as part of the common in 1968.

On 14th June 2021, the North Yorkshire County Council, Planning and Regulatory Functions Sub-Committee, met to consider the application from the Burgage Pastures Committee (BPC). Members of the Planning Committee agreed to recommend to the Chief Executive to grant the application. If approved then the official register will be amended, meaning that the racecourse buildings will no longer be part of the Common.

It is hoped that this action might help the BPC find a workable solution for the preservation and possible repurposing of these historic buildings.

Part 3
THE MILITARY ON THE RACECOURSE

Officers from the (Alexandra Princess of Wales Own) or Yorkshire Hussars relaxing on the racecourse in 1910

There is a long and proud tradition of the racecourse, its buildings and the surrounding site being used by the military that goes back to before race meetings ended in 1891 and continued until Gallowgate Army Camp was deemed surplus to military requirements by the War Department and closed in the early 1960s. It was as recently as September 1991 that Richmond's nuclear monitoring post, sited on the edge of the old racecourse, was finally stood down.

The Volunteers, later the Territorials, held summer camps on the racecourse (usually in July) for two weeks each year. It was commonly used by men of the Territorials of the 4th Battalion of the Yorkshire

Regiment (as the Green Howards were then known) with Richmond contributing a company of men. The camps attempted to prepare the 'Terriers' for what life in the field might be like, so they practised pitching tents, cooking with field kit, repairing kit, marching with the band, training with equipment such as the Maxim gun and playing cricket. The camp ended with a full review of the men attending.

4th Battalion Yorkshire Regiment of the Territorials camping on the racecourse early 1890's

Although the *Leeds Mercury* described how the Richmond racecourse camp had a glorious setting, commanding views of 50 miles, the annual camps on the exposed site were not always a pleasurable experience. The weather could be extreme, even in summer. In 1891, Volunteers from the 3rd Durham Light Infantry (Sunderland) were under canvas at Richmond Racecourse. The weather was absolutely foul, with cold and torrential rain, when a bugler named Kirby became lost and fell into a limestone quarry. He badly gashed his head and lay there for three days, his head covered in blood and his eyesight damaged, before recovering enough to stagger back into the camp by Low Gingerfield Farm. His cap and stick were subsequently found in the quarry. The stones around were covered in blood. Dr Burns of Sunderland was able to pay every attention to his serious scalp injuries. Although, initially, only slight hopes were entertained for his recovery, Kirby did survive and his eyesight recovered.

Just two years later, in July 1893, the *Richmond and Ripon Chronicle* reported that the army camp on the racecourse had been struck by lightning during a thunderstorm and five soldiers were injured.

Robert (later Lord) Baden-Powell, as General Officer Commanding Northern Territorial Army 1908-1910, oversaw an expansion in scale of the camps on the racecourse. The *Leeds Mercury* of Saturday 3 July 1909 reported that the 4th Battalion (Northallerton) and 5th Battalion (Scarborough) of the Yorkshire Regiment of Territorials was to proceed to the camp on Richmond Racecourse as part of the York and Durham Division of the Northumbrian Brigade. There would be about 3,000 men and officers in camp under the command of Colonel Eccles.

On 21 June 1910 it was reported that 4,000 soldiers from the Northumberland Brigade of the Territorials camped on the racecourse. The lines extended the whole length of the course, with an open space in the middle, in which there was ample room for drilling.

Officers inspecting the troops at the Richmond Camp

Throughout the afternoon and early evening the ordinarily peaceful streets of Richmond echoed to the rattle of drums, the shrill call of bugles and the tramp of armed men, as detachment after detachment de-trained at the station and marched away up the hillside. The weather was gloriously fine, the men finding their marching equipment a heavy burden in the summer sunshine. An interesting feature of the Richmond camp was the presence of two squadrons of Hussars.

The Yorkshire Hussars in front of the impressive Grandstand

Enjoying a beer

With so many troops assembled on the racecourse, arrangements had to be made for provisions and activities when not in training. The *Leeds Mercury* reported how water had to be piped from the Victoria Reservoir to tanks at the bottom of the racecourse. Arrangements also had to be made for sport, music and general entertainment.

Annual training camps continued in the years between the wars, despite the development of Catterick Garrison by this time. In June 1933 the Yorkshire Hussars completed one week's training on the racecourse and were rewarded by a social gathering organised by the Richmond Chamber of Trade.

Drum Head Service at the Richmond Camp

4th Battalion band 1910

By the time of the Great War, the camps on the racecourse had become a preparation for combat.

4th Yorkshire Regiment standing easy

Checking and inspecting tack

Between 1940 and 1945 the racecourse and grandstand were used for different purposes. In 1944 the grandstand was leased to the RAF for office/storeroom accommodation. To facilitate this use, the Borough removed the brickwork with which it had blocked up the doorways and large arched openings. The brickwork was put back when the RAF ceased its tenancy in 1945. There is anecdotal evidence from older Richmond folk of the grandstand being used for dances during the war. Barbara Annabelle Peacock of Hurgill Lodge remembers the building being affectionately known as Blessam or Bless'em Hall. One elderly gent, encountered whilst walking on the racecourse, described what a marvellous dance floor there was in the grandstand. These were clearly happy memories!

The racecourse was also used for training the Local Defence Volunteers. Popularly known as the Home Guard, they were lightly armed and trained for the expected invasion. They also had the role of capturing German airmen shot down in the local area.

The Royal Observer Corps

Before, during and after WW2, Richmond Racecourse, situated high above the town and with a commanding 360-degree view, was an important site for the Royal Observer Corps. The grandstand itself was used throughout WW2 as an observation point. Of greater long-term significance, however, was the siting of a Royal Observer Corps Post just to the south of the Whashton Road car park.

The first post on this site opened in December 1936 as part of 9 Group, which covered the North Riding of Yorkshire. It would have been a simple affair, made up of sandbags and corrugated iron sheets. Its role was to act as a reporting point for tracking aircraft flying in a 10-mile radius around the post. For the duration of WW2 it would have been manned 24 hours a day.

Observer 16164, Harry Metcalfe, joined the Richmond Post in 1940. One of his wartime memories is of the Richmond Post being the first to correctly identify the Northrop P-61 Black Widows when they arrived at Scorton. Other posts had plotted these distinctive aircraft as German Fw 189s as they flew the length of the country to reach the base. Harry also recounts spotting a Dakota, and sending a report to York, by phone, where he heard a party and singing. This, he claimed, was the last plane spotted by the ROC during WW2, as peace had just been declared.

Towards the end of WW2, Richmond Post, along with other posts on the high ground of the Pennines, such as Leyburn, served as a 'Granite Post', equipped with red flares, which could be lit to warn any low flying aircraft in danger of flying into high ground. The post was part of Operation Granite that successfully reduced the numbers of RAF fatalities in the final years of the war.

A Beaufort V8452 had crashed in Richmond on 14 December 1942. It was one of three scrambled from Scorton airfield to intercept a number of Luftwaffe aircraft when the pilot reported that he had lost control. It is thought that a tail plane weather cover had been left on the plane, making it impossible for the pilot to prevent the crash. Narrowly missing the fire-watch lookout on the castle keep, the plane crashed into a small field on Bolton Crofts, just south of the racecourse. Despite the heroic efforts of several locals, the pilot and his Flight Sergeant both died in the crash.

Beaufort V8452

Around 1943, the post was provided with a much more suitable two-storey brick-built observation tower. This structure had a rest room, with beds on the ground floor and facilities for cooking. An external ladder led up to the observation platform on the second floor, manned by two observers and equipped with a post plotting instrument and chart. Around the top were glass panels, which could give some protection to the observers on duty.

The post was stood down on 12 May 1945, at the end of WW2, but was reopened on 1 January 1947 when the Corps was given a low-level aircraft intruder role in the early days of the Cold War. The observers were now part-time. In 1955, the Royal Observer Corps was given the role of monitoring the nuclear threat and radioactive fallout. Its aircraft-reporting role was gradually phased out. In line with this new role, posts such as that at Richmond were provided with underground nuclear bunkers. Richmond's bunker was built adjoining the former two-storey aircraft reporting tower and was opened in September 1962 as part of 23 Group Durham. In 1982, the post was once again re-designated, this time as a Master Post to aid electronic transmission of data for the Cluster with Group Control.

On 30 September 1991, Richmond's post was finally stood down by the Government in the changing political climate brought about by the collapse of communism in Russia and the thawing of the Cold War. Today, there are no signs of the 1943 two-storey observation tower, which was demolished around 1962. Remains of the nuclear post can, however, still be seen close to a radio mast. It remains as a legacy of the tensions of the post-WW2 era and the continued role played by the Richmond racecourse site. For those readers who are interested in the spine-chilling secret history of the Cold War era, English Heritage has converted an actual Cold War bunker that can be visited at York.

The role of the racecourse site in training soldiers also continued well after the end of WW2.

Gallowgate Camp

It was during WW2, in 1940 and 1941, that the Gallowgate Army Camp was built as an overspill for the Green Howards Barracks. After the war it was used as a training ground for the Royal Signals during the time of National Service, before finally being declared surplus to requirements by the War Department in the late 1950s and closed in the early 1960s.

Local historian Mike Wood remembers the Open Days that were held by the Green Howards for local people in the early 1950s. The highlight for children was a ride in a Bren Gun carrier and the recovery of an army wagon from the old quarry on the side of the racecourse. To add to the enjoyment, they also gave out bars of chocolate in plain brown wrappers. Chocolate was still rationed at the time.

The buildings of the camp were mostly single-storey wood and brick huts. Many of the huts were flat roofed and built with bricks on the edge. Anecdotal evidence is that the builder, nicknamed 'Bricks on the edge Reg', and his Clerk of Works saved thousands of bricks by using this method. The surplus bricks were then sold on the black market, though it is reported that both men ended up in jail as a result of their scam. The building shown on page 72 was situated behind the guard room, where the Royal Mail is now sited. Note the bricks on the edge. Housing up to 1,000 soldiers and with no insulation, the main concern for the troops was to keep warm!

In the early 1960s, the camp was described in the North Riding of Yorkshire Development Plan thus: 'Gallowgate Camp lies at a height of between 675 and 775 feet above sea level on an area of hard limestone on the north side of the town of Richmond. The total area of the Camp is some 39 acres. The Camp is approached via Gallowgate and Green Howards Road and the camp entrance is situated at the junction of the Green Howards Road and Quarry Road. The Camp consists of 96 buildings of wood and brick, generally of single storey, although some are up to 25 ft in height. As the Camp is visible from the skyline from Richmond Castle and from many parts of the town, it is important that all redundant buildings shall be removed to ensure that the distant prospect of the Camp is screened as far as possible and not marred by any new development.'

Guard duty with pick axe handle, 1956

KIND PERMISSION – MR J WOODHOUSE

Two-storey ROC post at Great Offley, in 17 Group Watford, 1943. Richmond's second wartime post would have looked like this.

KIND PERMISSION – ROYAL OBSERVER CORPS

Richmond Borough Council was keen to develop the site for light industry once it was declared surplus by the War Department. In 1962 the Council was given permission by North Riding Planning to purchase 28 acres for approximately £10,000. Some 10 acres were to be cleared and a further 10 acres returned to the original owners, including two fields sold back to a local farmer, Malcolm Firby. Some of the redundant buildings around the old parade ground, now Mercury Road, were removed and plots sold relatively cheaply. As recently as the late 1960s, the estate was partly agricultural, with pigs and horses being housed in buildings in Borough Road, but it began to develop as a trading estate when Fairfield Shoe Factory was built on Racecourse Road in 1967-8. Further businesses followed, especially after agreement between the District and County Councils to improve the roads in 1980. Today, the site of the former barracks houses around 100 successful and prosperous businesses. The vision of the Borough Council to have light industry established in the old army camp adjacent to the racecourse has been fully vindicated.

Troops assembled on Mercury Road parade ground

"Smile Lads" – Soldiers at Gallowgate Camp

Part 4
RICHMOND BURGAGE PASTURES COMMITTEE

'Burgage' is a form of tenure applicable to property connected with the old municipal Corporations such as Richmond. The term was well established by the thirteenth century, though it may date back to pre-Norman times. These houses were typically grouped round the market place and consisted of a narrow street frontage with a long, narrow plot of land at the back. The owners of the burgage houses held certain privileges and rights. Whilst most of the older houses in Richmond enjoyed these rights, not all did so. On occasion this could lead to dissent, as the privileges could be a source of income and influence.

A traditional right was to pasture, or 'stint', the owners' cattle on various designated open spaces outside the town. Whitcliffe Pasture, an area of some 940 acres that came to be the site of the racecourse, was one such 'stinted pasture'. The Pasture Master was responsible for ensuring that any regulations and restrictions concerning the stinting were adhered to, and that the correct number of cattle were put out to pasture.

A much coveted right that was later 'added on' to that of stinting, was the right to vote in parliamentary elections. It was for this reason that the first official list of burgage houses in Richmond was made in 1679, in the lead up to the General Election of that year. Effectively, this list of burgage houses was an electoral roll, but it remained unclear as to whether the term 'burgess' referred to the owners or to the occupiers of the burgage houses. In 1727, following a disputed election which brought into question who exactly had the right to vote, it was confirmed by a House of Commons committee that the votes for Richmond's two MPs were vested in the owners of its 273 burgage houses. Consequently, anyone who owned 137 of these houses could, therefore, control the election of Richmond's MPs and make it a 'Pocket Borough'. (The election of the MP was said to be in the pocket of whoever controlled the votes).

The Richmond Burgage Committee records for 23/24 February 1760 report 'the sale by Rt Hon Robert Earl of Holderness to Sir Lawrence Dundas of Upleatham Hall Cleveland of 131 Burgage Houses in Richmond for £30,000'. Sir Lawrence Dundas then bought Aske and its estate from Lord Holderness for £45,000 in the winter of 1762/3. Within a short time, the total of houses with burgage rights that he owned had risen to 163, thus making Richmond a Pocket Borough. In 1773, Sir Lawrence commissioned a 'Plan of the Borough of Richmond in Yorkshire' showing every house in the town, with or without burgage rights. Those burgage houses he already owned were coloured black. Those owned by John Yorke Esq were coloured brown. Those that it might be possible to acquire were coloured red. Richmond remained a Pocket Borough until the 1832 Parliamentary Reform Act, at which time the number of these seats was significantly reduced.

As horse racing developed in Richmond, so the ancient right of stinting on Whitcliffe Pasture and the role of the Pasture Master overlapped with the role of the Corporation and the racehorse owners and trainers. There appears to have been an element of shared responsibility, with the Corporation responsible for organising the races and appointing the stewards, while the accounts of the Pasture Master refer to costs involved in course repairs and erecting temporary scaffolding. The situation was, however, both complex and subject to disagreement, as suggested in the preamble to the 1802 Enclosure Act. This Act enclosed much of the old open fields around Richmond, such as Gallow Field, but most of the original West Field, together with that part of Whitcliffe Pasture which had become the racecourse, was left as open spaces, still subject to burgage rights. This did little to clarify the precise nature of ownership of the land.

In 1853 the Richmond (Yorkshire) Burgage Pastures Act removed the right of individual burgage owners to graze their animals on the racecourse. The management of the rights was vested in the Burgage Pastures Committee. The Committee, consisting of nine burgage owners, has continued to meet annually since 1853 and appoint a Pasture Master to manage its affairs. Under the 1853 Act the Committee also gained the right to lease the land for up to one year and to hold rents and profits from the race meetings in trust for the 'owners of the ancient burgage houses'.

The 1853 Act, however, only served to continue the confusion of rights of ownership over the racecourse site. At the same time as recognising the role of the Burgage Pastures Committee in managing the historic burgage rights, the Act reaffirmed the Borough's interest in the site. It stated that the Mayor and Aldermen of the Borough of Richmond claimed that the land, soil and buildings of the Burgage Pastures were seised (in the legal possession) of the Borough for the use and benefit of certain inhabitants of the Borough, *except that the rights 'held and enjoyed' by the owners of the Burgage Houses (*some of whom, such as Lord Dundas, were named*) were to be protected*. In other words, the Act confirmed that there were conflicting claims.

These conflicting claims were not to be resolved until 2008, when the mantle of ownership of the racecourse and its buildings, its subsoil and its woodland was handed over by the Richmondshire District Council to the Burgage Pastures Committee.

Since 1892, once the race meetings had ended, the Burgage Pastures Committee continued to receive income from fees charged to trainers and owners for the use of the racecourse and gallops. By the early twentieth century, this income had severely reduced, with fewer horses using the site. One of the last to use the gallops for her horses and pay fees was Mrs Muriel Naughton of High Gingerfield. Because the racecourse contains much unimproved pasture land, the Committee also received an income to manage the land under a Stewardship Scheme.

In this way, the Richmond Burgage Pastures Committee has held a long standing interest in the maintenance and management of the racecourse. Part 2 of this book, on the fight to save the grandstand, tells the story of how the Committee intervened to help save the grandstand from demolition in 1969-70 and, in 2008, received full ownership of the racecourse and its buildings from the Richmondshire District Council.

The Committee's legacy of involvement over the centuries also helps the reader to understand its efforts since 2008 to improve the site and to restore and re-purpose the grandstand as a unique landmark in the history of horse racing, both locally and nationally.

Title page – Act of Parliament – 1853

ACKNOWLEDGEMENTS AND SOURCES

The Burgage Pastures Committee is indebted to Professor Huggins, who was first contacted by Committee member Donald Cline, for his original work. Graham Berry, former Head of History at Richmond School, has checked and written up the stories and other material which have been added to Professor Huggins's work. The researched material used for the stories and the more recent history was mainly uncovered by Colin Grant, a former Pasture Master, and Mike Wood, both members of the Burgage Pastures Committee. Mike inherited, and was able to draw on, Ralph Waggett's extensive archive about the history of Richmond Racecourse. Ralph was a former Chairman of the Committee. We should also like to mention the contribution by Barbara Annabel Brown, who, with failing health, provided many memories to Aileen Monkhouse, Harry Peacock's granddaughter and of Linda Turnbull at the County Records Office, who helped research many of the historical details in the lead-up to her retirement. Proofreading has been undertaken by numerous individuals including Jane McLennan and Nina Cline.

The account by Professor Huggins has been referenced in the Endnotes which follow.

Other sources of research information have been the Burgage Pastures Minute Books; Richmond Corporation Coucher Books; the North Yorkshire County Archives; the Earl of Ronaldshay and the Marquess of Zetland; Jane Hatcher's *History of Richmond* and *Richmondshire Architecture*; the Richmond Racecourse Conservation Management Plan; the National Newspaper Archive; J. Fairfax-Blakeborough's *Northern Turf History*; Ministry of Defence; Royal Observer Corps; The British Museum; York Racecourse; National Horseracing Museum, Newmarket; Richmond and District Civic Society, *Millennium Review*; Robert Graves, *They Hung My Saintly Billy*, and Audrey Carr, *You Must Remember This*.

Images and material have also been provided by Jane Hatcher; Carl Watts from the Green Howards Museum; Richmondshire Museum; the Georgian Theatre Royal archive; Chris Lloyd; Alan Gilpin; Barbara Brown; Stuart Parsons; Jim Jack; Mike Wood; and Colin Grant.

The information for the Introduction, the Snow Tankard and Parts 2-4 of the book by Graham, Colin and Mike was gathered in a year with three Covid lock downs, when many archival institutions were shut to the public. At the time of going to print, this information is, to the best of our knowledge, correct. We hope that along with the authoritative expertise of Professor Mike Huggins, we have gathered sufficient for you to have enjoyed reading this fascinating short history.

ENDNOTES

The site of race meetings on the High Moor

Although there are many references to racing taking place on the High Moor before 1765, the actual location of the site remains uncertain. It is known that the entrance to the High Moor site lay along the old road to Marske, close to the Sun Inn (near to Beacon Cottage today), but there are two adjacent High Moors, both of which still bear that name today. One lies to the south of the Marske road on the common land leading towards Willance's Leap. The other lies to the north of the Marske road, about a mile north-west of the Beacon. Both can lay claim to be the site where racing took place before the move to the Low Moor course.

Professor Huggins believes that racing probably took place on the turf of the High Moor to the north of the high road to Marske. This area is easily accessed along a walled Bridleway which starts by Beacon Cottage, close to where the old Sun Inn stood. Support for the site is offered by the existence of a Rubbing House, now a domestic dwelling with that name, between this High Moor and the nearby Out Moor. Such a building is usually a good indication of where racing and gallops took place on moorland areas. Tall doorways allowed the horses to be ridden straight in. They would be well wrapped - up while sweating after their gallop before they were then rubbed down. Another possible clue to this site being where the races took place is 'Jockey Cap clump', the name given to a prominent group of trees on a hill overlooking the High Moor.

There is, however, another High Moor to the south of the old Marske Road which has traditionally laid claim to being the site of the original racecourse! This too could be accessed along a track between two walls which began close to the old Sun Inn and was where the Richmond historian, Ralph Waggett, always believed that the course lay. It is this High Moor that continued to be controlled by the Burgage Pastures Committee and was clearly labelled as 'High Moor' on a map that was brought to its meetings. It is also this High Moor site that was used by Harry Peacock on which to train his Hurgill Lodge horses. There are many in Richmond who have always assumed that it was on this site, to the south of the Marske Road, that racing took place before 1765.

Sources from the period that refer to the High Moor race course are both few in number and vague in detail. The diary of an unknown Richmond woman (*Life in Georgian Richmond: A Diary and its Secrets* by Jane Hatcher and Bob Woodings 2018), simply describes travelling up to the 'High Moor' to see the races. Clarkson's *History of Richmond* (1821) has one tantalising reference that states 'In 1741 the Lime Kilns near the Race Ground were let upon leave for seven years by the Corporation to Thomas Watkin'. In 1741, the 'Race Ground' would still have been the High Moor site, but Clarkson does not say which lime kilns he was referring to. There were several places between Marske and Richmond where lime kilns could be found, including Coalsgarth and Gingerfield, such that a case could be made from this source for either racecourse site. Without further definitive evidence, it is difficult today to be certain which High Moor was the site of the original race meetings. Perhaps this is not surprising, given that early racing sites were not well-defined. Each year, as described by Christopher Clarkson, a course would be laid out on the moor with some white tapes, such that you were not limited as to where precisely nor even how long the course was.

The Snow Tankard race

Although the Borough records give a date of 1686 for the running of the Snow Tankard race, recent research has suggested that it may actually have been run some years later, albeit still on the High Moor site. There are two reasons for this interpretation.

Firstly, the period around 1686 does not match a time when there were two squires fitting the names and descriptions inscribed on the tankard. A time around 1755 would better fit with the existence of Sir Mark Milbank, John Hutton senior and, by implication, an adult John Hutton junior.

Secondly, an entry in the Corporation Chamberlain's Accounts states that 'Dec. ye 19 1755 The Corp'n of Rd. Dr. to Michael Waggitt For engraving 48 letters on a large silver Tankard belonging to ye Corporation called the Snow Tankard £0 4s 0d. (Receipted and Signed) Mich'l. Waggitt'. This translates that, on 19th December 1755, the Corporation of Richmond, debtor to Michael Waggitt (a Richmond clock and watchmaker), paid 4 shillings (80p) for engraving 48 letters on the Snow Tankard. It would be reasonable to expect that the engraving took place soon after the race and the donation of the Snow Tankard to the Corporation.

Snow tankard – on display at Green Howards Museum

FOOTNOTES

1. *Newcastle Chronicle, 9 March 1776.*

2. *Robin Wragg, The Life and Works of John Carr of York: Palladian Architect Vols 1-3 (Sheffield: UOS, 1976).*

3. *North Yorkshire Record office, Richmond Coucher Book, CR0NT 1520.*

4. *North Yorkshire Record office, Richmond Coucher Book, CR0NT 1520.*

5. *David Oldrey, Timothy Cox and Richard Nash, The Heath and the Horse: A History of Racing and Art on Newmarket Heath (London: PWP, 2016)*

6. *Paul Roberts and Isabel Taylor, Racecourse Architecture (Turnbury Consulting and acanthus Press, 2013), a generally good overview, fails to recognise Wakefield's role*

7. *Mark Hallett and Jane Rendall, Eighteenth Century York: Culture, Space and Society (York: Borthwick Institute, 2003), pp.1-12; Paul Roberts and Isabel Taylor, Racecourse Architecture (Turnbury Consulting and acanthus Press, 2013), a generally good overview, fails to recognise Wakefield's role.*

8. *Poulson, George: Beverlac, or The Antiquities and History of the Town of Beverley. (Beverley, Longman, Rees, Orme, Brown, & Green, 1829), p. 449.*

9. *See engraving by R G Reeve from a painting Francis Calcraft Turner, Heaton Park Races 1835*

10. *R G Reeve from a painting by Francis Calcraft Turner, Ascot Heath Races 1835; J.F. Herring, The Doncaster Gold Cup of 1838.*

11. *Christopher Clarkson, A History of Richmond in the County of York (Richmond: Bowman, 1821), p.281.*

12. *York Herald, 12 May 1883; York Herald 30 June 1883; York Herald 14 July 1883*

13. *Yorkshire Gazette, 30 August 1884.*

14. *See for example J. Fairfax-Blakeborough, Northern Turf History Vol.1, Hambleton and Richmond (London: J A Allen 1948), p.296.*

15. *North Yorkshire Record Office, Richmond Racing Papers DC/RMB.*

16. *York Herald, 1 September 1883*

17. *Yorkshire Gazette, 30 August 1884.*

18. *York Herald, 2 February 1805*

19. *See Richard Nash, 'Beware a Bastard Breed': Notes Toward a Revisionist History of the Thoroughbred Racehorse', in The Horse as Cultural Icon: The Real and Symbolic Horse in The Early Modern world ed Peter Edwards, Karl Enenkel and Elspeth Graham Leiden: Brill 2012, pp 101-216*

20. *Daniel Defoe, Journeys Round England Book 2 letter VIII, pp. 220-21.*

21. *See Joyce Kay, 'Closing the Stable Door and the Public Purse: The Rise and Fall of the Royal Plates', Sports Historian, 20:1, 2003, pp. 18-32*

22. *John Cheny, A Historical List of All Horsematches Run and of all Plates and Prizes Run for in 1728 (London: cheny, 1828).*

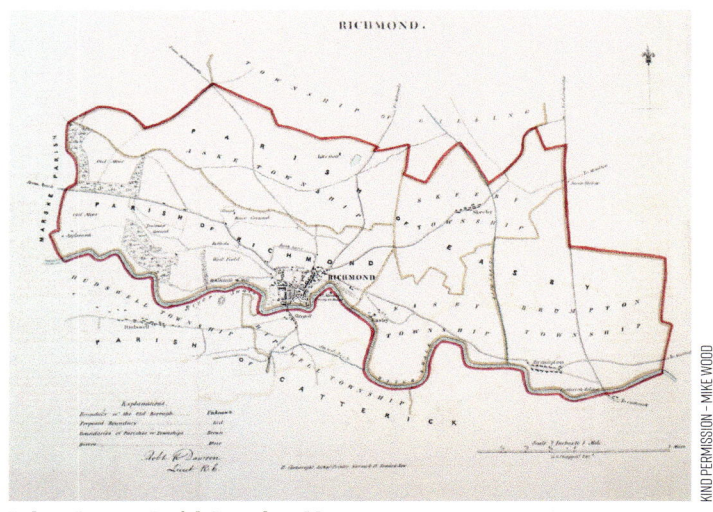

Robert Dawson Parish Boundary Map 1831

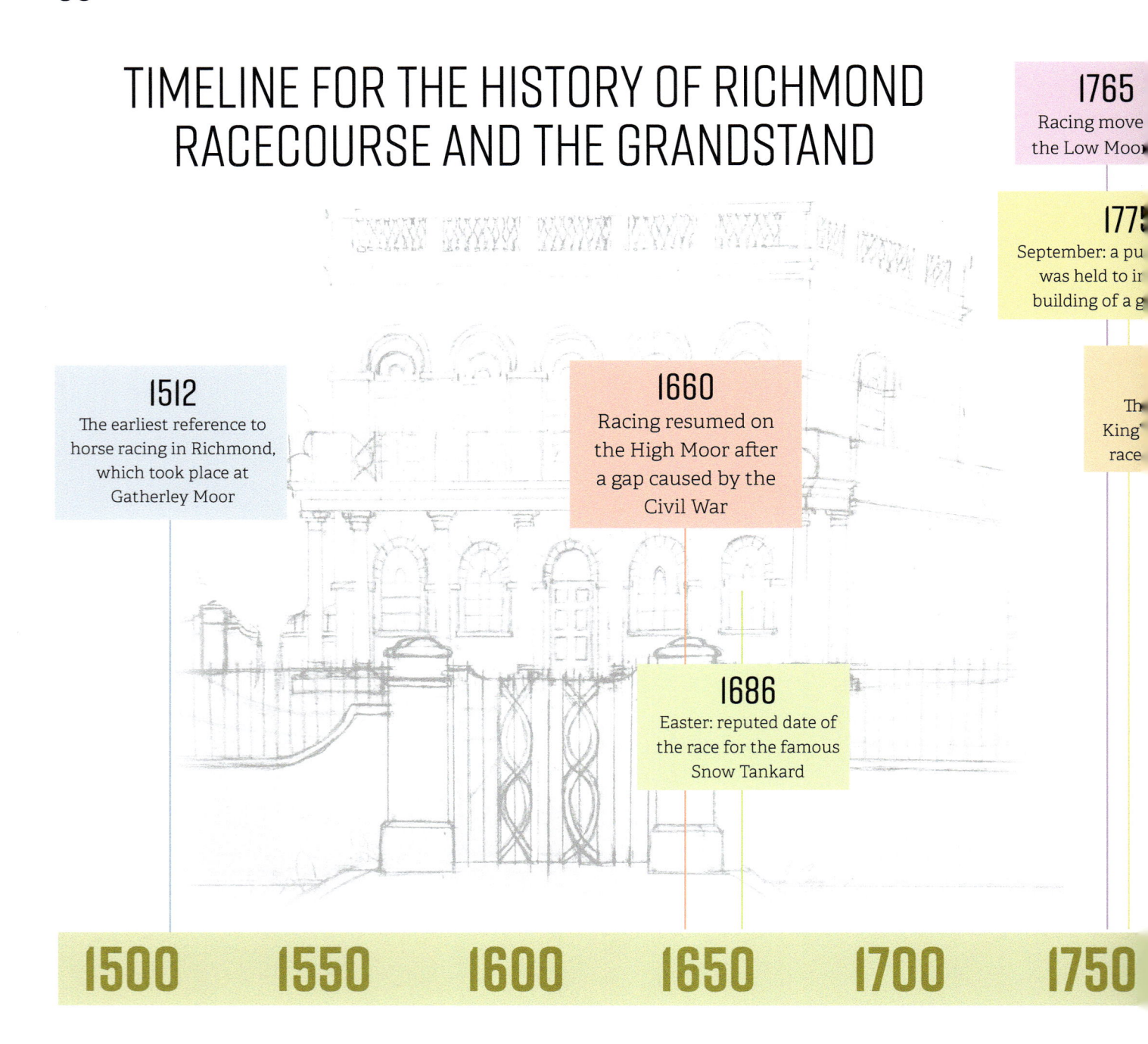

TIMELINE FOR THE HISTORY OF RICHMOND RACECOURSE AND THE GRANDSTAND

1512 — The earliest reference to horse racing in Richmond, which took place at Gatherley Moor

1660 — Racing resumed on the High Moor after a gap caused by the Civil War

1686 — Easter: reputed date of the race for the famous Snow Tankard

1765 — Racing move the Low Moor

1775 — September: a pu was held to ir building of a g

Th King race

1500 — 1550 — 1600 — 1650 — 1700 — 1750

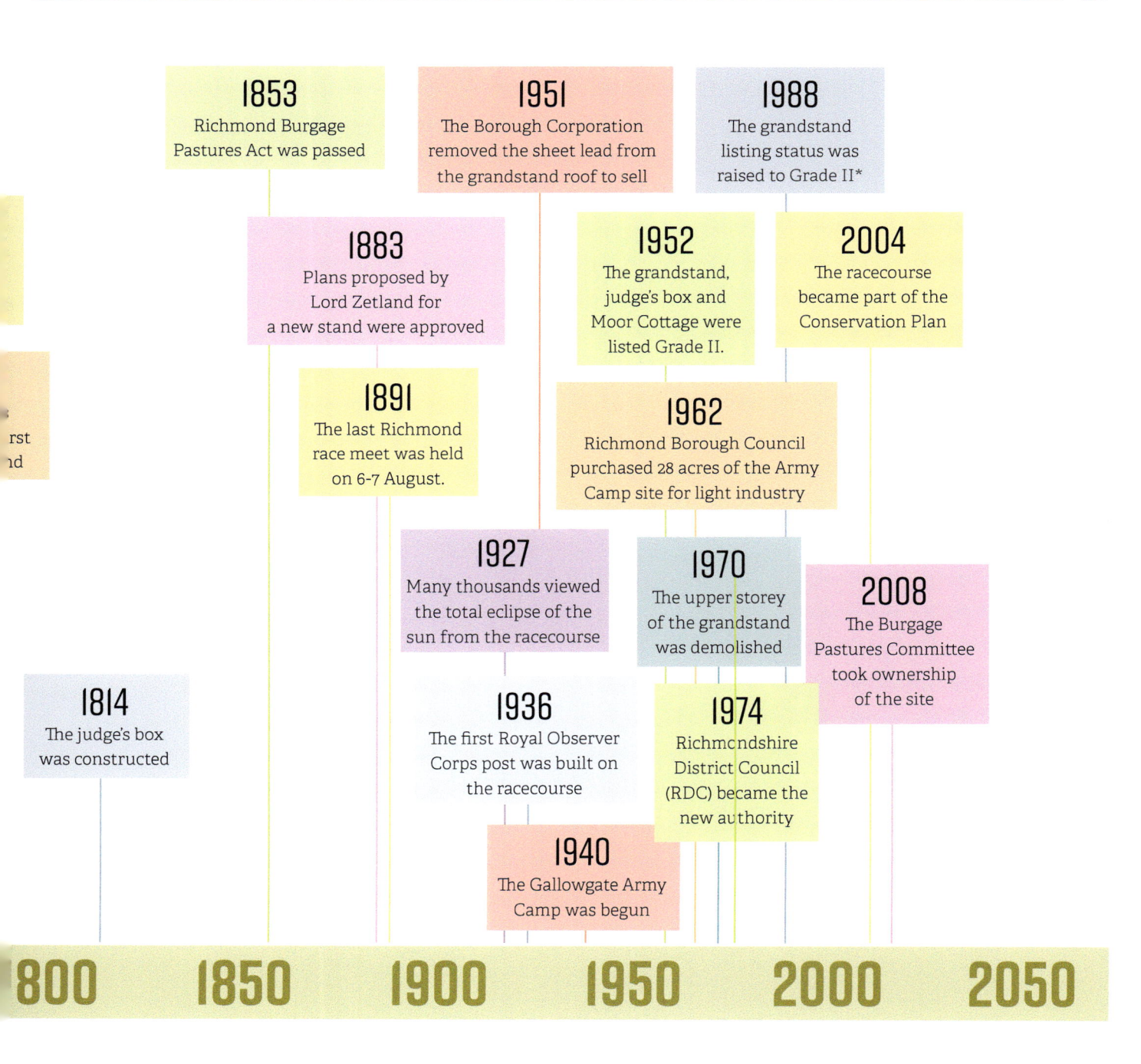

A SHORT HISTORY OF RICHMOND RACECOURSE AND ITS GRANDSTAND

Timeline

- **1814** — The judge's box was constructed
- **1853** — Richmond Burgage Pastures Act was passed
- **1883** — Plans proposed by Lord Zetland for a new stand were approved
- **1891** — The last Richmond race meet was held on 6-7 August.
- **1927** — Many thousands viewed the total eclipse of the sun from the racecourse
- **1936** — The first Royal Observer Corps post was built on the racecourse
- **1940** — The Gallowgate Army Camp was begun
- **1951** — The Borough Corporation removed the sheet lead from the grandstand roof to sell
- **1952** — The grandstand, judge's box and Moor Cottage were listed Grade II.
- **1962** — Richmond Borough Council purchased 28 acres of the Army Camp site for light industry
- **1970** — The upper storey of the grandstand was demolished
- **1974** — Richmondshire District Council (RDC) became the new authority
- **1988** — The grandstand listing status was raised to Grade II*
- **2004** — The racecourse became part of the Conservation Plan
- **2008** — The Burgage Pastures Committee took ownership of the site